THE SCIENCE AND PHILOSOPHY OF RELIGION

THE SCIENCE AND PHILOSOPHY OF RELIGION:

A COMPARATIVE STUDY OF SANKHYA, VEDANTA AND OTHER SYSTEMS OF THOUGHT

SWAMI VIVEKANANDA

GYAN

Published by

Gyan Publishing House
5, Ansari Road
Daryaganj, New Delhi-110002
Phone: 011-47034999, 9811692060
E-mail: books@gyanbooks.com

Distribution Network
gyanbooks.com
India, USA, Canada, UK, Australia

ISBN: 978-93-7014-032-5 (HB)

First Published, 1908

2nd Impression 2025

Printed at: Gyan Press, Delhi.

THE SCIENCE AND PHILOSOPHY OF RELIGION
Author: SWAMI VIVEKANANDA

THE

SCIENCE AND PHILOSOPHY OF RELIGION

(A COMPARATIVE STUDY OF SANKHYA, VEDANTA AND OTHER SYSTEMS OF THOUGHT)

BY

SWAMI VIVEKANANDA

1908.

EDITOR'S PREFACE.

"When any Science reaches a unity, it cannot possibly go any farther. You cannot go beyond this idea of the Absolute, the idea of the One, out of which everything in the universe has evolved. * * The last word of Advaita is *Tattvamasi*,—That thou art." These are the words of the author of the present volume, at the end of the book. It is a clear and concise statement of the daring claim made by the Sages of India, from very old times, that they have attained to such Unity in the religious field and succeeded in bringing Religion to the rank of a perfect and complete Science. The methods adopted by them to come to this result, were the same as followed by all the Sciences of the present day, *viz.*, observation and analysis of the facts of our experience, and a synthetical combination of the results obtained, to find out the same facts. That Kapila, Vyasa, Patanjali and indeed all the philosophers of India, including most of the Vedic Seers, applied these methods in coming to their respective discoveries—has been fully discussed by the author in his books on the different Yogas.

Wonderful as the claim seems and improbable to the Superficial eye, the world had not had the power and inclination to shift the grounds on which it was advanced. The difficulties of an obsolete language, expression and imagery, the two concise character of the aphorisms (Sutras) and the leaden dross of time always overwhelmed or led astray the stray stragglers, who made any attempt along the line while the Indian national mind was sleeping through centuries, perfectly exhausted with the super-human exertions of the great discovery! No wonder it needed the present period of reawakening of 'the mother-land of Dharma' and along with it the Superhuman vision of Bhagawan Sri Ramakrishna and the gifted talent of Swami Vivekananda to do the work as well as to teach humanity the way to apply the great truth to its daily life, in India and abroad—for an Indian mind is always needed to interpret things purely Indian. To understand fully the greatness of the Swami, however, we must always bear in mind the fact that these were a Series of seven lectures, delivered without notes, before a little class in New York, in the beginning of 1896! It is fortunate indeed, that they were taken down at the time by shorthand, making it possible for us to get them printed in this present form, after the expiration of such a long time and the editor is thankful for being requested to do his work while he was in America, at the beginning of 1897.

Editor's Preface.

Nothing of any importance has been changed in the body of the lectures themselves excepting the substitution of the word *Prakriti* for Nature. In the editor's humble opinion there is no English equivalent for the Sanskrit word and Nature can never be one. For the idea connoted by it is the finished result of what is connoted by the word *Prakriti*. *Prakriti* therefore can never mean Nature but the primal elements and forces, which form the materials for the creation of the universe. *Prakriti* is the cause, of which Nature is the effect or out of which Nature is being produced. "Primal matter and energy held in equilibrium" or "the latent condition of primal matter and energy" expresses the idea aright. We would request the reader to keep this will stamped in his mind to understand the words of the Swami in the following pages clearly.

CONTENTS.

CONTENTS

INTRODUCTION

THIS universe of ours, the universe of the senses, the rational, the intellectual, is bounded on both sides by the illimitable, the unknowable, the ever unknown. Herein is the search, herein are the inquiries, here are the facts, whence comes the light which is known to the world as religion. Essentially, however, religion belongs to the supersensuous and not to the sense plane. It is beyond all reasoning and is not on the plane of intellect. It is a vision, an inspiration, a plunge into the unknown and unknowable, making the unknowable more than known, for it can never be "known." The search has been in the human mind, as I believe, from the very beginning of humanity. There cannot have been human reasoning and intellect in any period of the world's history without this struggle, this search beyond. In our little universe, the human mind, we see a thought arise. Whence it arises we do not know, and when it disappears, where it goes we know not either. The macrocosm and the microcosm are, as it were, in the same groove, passing through the same stages, vibrating in the same key.

In these lectures I shall try to bring before you the Hindu theory that religions do not come from without, but from within. It is my belief that religious thought is in man's very constitution, so much so that it is impossible for him to give up religion until he can give up his mind and body, until he can give up thought and life. As long as a man thinks, this struggle must go on, and so long man must have some form of religion. Thus we see various forms of religion in the world.

It is a bewildering study, but it is not, as many of us think, a vain speculation. Amidst this chaos there is harmony, throughout these discordant sounds there is a note of concord, and he who is prepared to listen to it will catch the tone.

The great question of all questions at the present time is this : Taking for granted that the known and the knowable are bounded on both sides by the unknowable and the infinitely unknown, why struggle for that infinite unknown ? Why shall we not be content with the known ? Why shall we not rest satisfied with eating, drinking, and doing a little good to society ? This idea is in the air. From the most learned professor to the prattling baby, we are told to do good to the world, that is all of religion, and that it is useless to trouble ourselves about questions of the beyond. So much is this the case that it has become a truism. But fortunately we *must* question the beyond. The present, the expressed, is only one part of that unexpressed. The sense universe is, as it were, only one portion, one bit of that infinite spiritual universe projected into the plane of sense consciousness. How can this little bit of projection be explained, be understood, without knowing that which is beyond? It is said of Socrates that one day while lecturing at Athens, he met a Brahmin who had travelled into Greece, and Socrates told the Brahmin that the greatest study for mankind is man. The Brahmin sharply retorted : "How can you know man until you know God?" This God, this eternally unknowable, or absolute, or infinite, or without name,—you may call Him by what name you like,—is the rational, the only explanation, the *raison d etre* of that which is known and knowable, this present life. Take anything before you, the most material thing ; take one of the most material sciences, as chemistry or physics, astronomy or biology, study it, push the study forward and forward, and the gross forms will begin to melt and become finer and finer, until they come to a point where you are bound to make a tremendous leap from these material things into the immaterial. The gross melts into the fine, physics into metaphysics, in every department of knowledge.

Thus man finds himself driven to a study of the beyond. Life will be a desert, human life will be vain if we cannot know the beyond. It is very well to say: Be contented with the things of the present; the cows and the dogs are, and all animals, and that is what makes them animals. So if man rests content with the present and gives up all search into the beyond, mankind will have to go back to the animal plane again. It is religion, the inquiry into the beyond, that makes the difference between man and an animal. Well has it been said that man is the only animal that naturally looks upwards ; every other animal naturally looks prone. That looking upward and going upward and seeking perfection are what is called salvation, and the sooner a man begins to go higher, the sooner he raises himself towards this idea of truth as salvation. It does not consist in the amount of money in your pocket, or the dress you wear, or the house you live in, but in the wealth of spiritual thought in your brain. That is what makes for human progress, that is the source of all material and intellectual progress, the motive power behind, the enthusiasm that pushes mankind forward.

Religion does not live in bread, does not dwell in a house. Again and again you hear this objection advanced, " What good can religion do ? Can it take away the provety of the poor ?" Supposing it cannot, would that prove the untruth of religion ?

Introduction

Suppose a baby stands up among you when you are trying to demonstrate an astronomical theorem, and says: "Does it bring gingerbread?" "No, it does not," you answer. "Then," says the baby, "it is useless." Babies judge the whole universe from their own standpoint, that of producing gingerbread, and so are the babies of the world. We must not judge of higher things from a low standpoint. Everything must be judged by its own standard and the infinite must be judged by an infinite standard. Religion permeates the whole of man's life, not only the present, but the past, present, and future. It is therefore the eternal relation between the eternal soul and the eternal God. Is it logical to measure its value by its action upon five minutes of human life? Certainly not. These are all negative arguments.

Now comes the question: Can religion really accomplish anything? It can. It brings to man eternal life. It has made man what he is and will make of this human animal a god. That is what religion can do. Take religion from human society and what will remain? Nothing but a forest of brutes. Sense-happiness is not the goal of humanity; wisdom (Jnânam) is the goal of all life. We find that man enjoys his intellect more than an animal enjoys its senses, and we see that man enjoys his spiritual nature even more than his rational nature. So the highest wisdom must be this spiritual knowledge. With this knowledge will come bliss. All these things of this world are but the shadows, the manifestations in the third or fourth degree of the real Knowledge and Bliss.

One question more: What is the goal? Nowadays it is asserted that man is infinitely progressing, forward and forward, and there is no goal of perfection to attain to.

Ever approaching, never attaining, whatever that may mean and however wonderful it may be, it is absurd on the face of it. Is there any motion in a straight line? A straight line infinitely projected becomes a circle, it returns to the starting point. You must end where you begin, and as you began in God, you must go back to God. What remains? Detail work. Through eternity you have to do the detail work.

Yet anther question. Are we to discover new truths of religion as we go on? Yea and nay. In the first place we cannot know anything more of religion, it has all been known. In all the religions of the world you will find it claimed that there is a unity within us. Being one with divinity, there cannot be any further progress in that sense. Knowledge means finding this unity. I see you as men and women, and this is variety. It becomes scientific knowledge when I group you together and call you human beings. Take the science of chemistry, for instance. Chemists are seeking to resolve all known substances into their original elements and if possible to find the one element from which all these were derived. The time may come when they will find one element that is the source of all other elements. Reaching that, they can go no farther ; the science of chemistry will have become perfect. So it is with the science of religion. If we can discover this perfect unity, there cannot be any farther progress.

The next question is : Can such a unity be found ? In India the attempt has been made from the earliest times to reach a science of religion and philosophy, for the Hindus do not separate these as is customary in Western countries. We regard religion and philosophy as but two aspects of one thing which must equally be grounded in reason and scientific truth. In the lectures that are to follow I shall try to explain to you first the system of the *Sânkhya* philosophy, one of the most ancient in India, or in fact in the world. Its great exponent Kapila is the father of all Hindu psychology and the ancient system that he taught is still the foundation of all accepted systems of philosophy in India to-day,—which are known as the *Dârsanas*. They all adopt his psychology, however widely they differ in other respects.

Next I shall endeavour to show you how Vedânta, as the logical outcome of the *Sânkhya*, pushes its conclusions yet farther. While its cosmology agrees with that taught by Kapila, the Vedânta is not satisfied to end in dualism, but continues its search for the final unity which is alike the goal of science and religion. To make clear the manner in which the task is accomplished will be the effort of the later lectures in this course.

I

THE SÂNKHYA COSMOLOGY

HERE are two words, the microcosm and the macrocosm, the internal and the external. We get truths from both of these by means of experience; there is internal experience and external experience. The truths gathered from internal experience are psychology, metaphysics and religion; from external experience the physical sciences. Now a perfect truth should be in harmony with experience in both these worlds. The microcosm must bear testimony to the macrocosm, and the macrocosm to the microcosm; physical truth must have its counterpart in the internal world, and the internal world must have its verification in the outside. Yet as a rule we find that many of these truths are constantly conflicting. At one period of the world's history the "internals" became supreme, and they began to fight the "externals" ; at the present time the "externals", the physicists, have become supreme, and they have put down many claims of the psychologists and metaphysicians. So far as my little knowledge goes, I find that the really essential parts of psychology are in perfect accordance with the essential parts of modern physical knowledge.

It is not given to every individual to be great in every respect ; it is not given to the same race, or nation, to be equally strong in the research of all the fields of knowledge. The modern European nations are very strong in their researches into external physical knowledge, but the ancient Europeans were weak in their researches into the internal part of man. On the other hand, the Orientals have not been very strong in their researches in the external physical world, but have excelled in their researches into the internal, and therefore we find that some of the Oriental theories are not in accordance with Occidental physics, neither is Occidental psychology in harmony with Oriental teachings on this subject. The Oriental physicists have been criticised by Occidental scientists. At the same time each rests on truth, and, as we stated before, real truth in any field of knowledge will not contradict itself, the truths internal are in harmony with the truths external.

We know the present theories of the Cosmos according to the modern astronomers and physicists, and at the same time we know how wofully they hurt the old school of theologians, and how every new scientific discovery that is made is as a bomb thrown into their house, and how they have attempted in every age to put down all these researches. In the first place, let us go over the psychological and scientific ideas of the Orientals as to cosmology and all that pertains to it, and you will find how wonderfully it is in accordance with all the latest discoveries of modern science, and when there is anything lacking you will find that it is on the side of modern science. We all use the word Nature, and the old Hindu philosophers called it by two different names, *Prakriti*, which is almost the same as the English word "nature", and by the more scientific name, *Avyaktam* ("undifferentiated"), from which everything proceeds, out of which come atoms and molecules, matter and force, and mind and intellect. It is startling to find that the philosophers and metaphysicians of India ages ago stated that mind is but matter in a finer form, for what are our present materialists striving to do but to show that mind is as much a product of nature as the body? And so is thought; and we shall find by and by that the intellect also comes from the same nature which is called *avyaktam*, the undifferentiated.

The ancient teachers define *avayaktam* as the "equilibrium of the three forces," one of which is called *Sattva*, the second *Rajas* and the third *Tamas*. *Tamas*, the lowest force, is that of attraction, a little higher is *Rajas*, that of repulsion, and the highest is the control of these two, *Sattva* : so that when the two forces, attraction and repulsion, are held in perfect control, or balance, by the *Sattva*, there is no creation, no modification ; but as soon as this equilibrium is lost, the balance is disturbed and one of these forces gets stronger than the other. Then change and motion begin and evolution of all this goes on. This state of things is going on cyclically, periodically ; that is to say, there is a period of disturbance of the balance, when all these forces begin to combine and recombine, and this universe is projected ; and there is also a period when everything has a tendency to revert to the primal state of equilibrium, and the time comes when a total absence of all manifestation is reached. Again, after a period, this state is disturbed, the forces tend to project outward and the universe slowly comes out in the form of waves; for all motion in this universe is in the form of waves, in successive rises and falls.

Some of the old philosophers taught that the whole universe quiets down for a period; others maintained that this quieting down applies only to systems. That is to say, that while our system here, this solar system, will quiet down and go back into that undifferentiated state, there will be millions of other systems going the other way. I should rather follow the second opinion, that this quieting down is not simultaneous over the whole universe, but that in different parts different things are going on. But the principle remains the same, that all that we see, that *Prakriti* herself is progressing in successive rises and falls. The stage of going back to the balance, to the perfect equilibrium, is called the end of a cycle. The whole *Kalpa*, the evolution and the involution, has been compared by theistic writers in India to the outbreathing and in-breathing of God ; God, as it were, breathes out the universe, and it returns into Him again. When it quiets down, what becomes of the universe? It still exists, only in finer form, as it is called in Sanskrit, in the "causal state" *(Kârana)*. Causation, time and space are still there, only they are potential. This return to an undifferentiated condition constitutes involution. Involution and evolution are eternally going on, so that when we speak of a beginning, we refer only to the beginning of a cycle.

The most extraneous part of the universe is what in modern times we call gross matter. The ancient Hindus called it the *Bhutas*, the external elements. One of these according to them is the cause of the rest for every other element is produced out of this one, and this element has been called *Âkâsa.* This is somewhat similar to the modern idea of ether, though not exactly the same. *Âkâsa* is the primal element out of which every gross thing proceeds, and along with it there is something else called *Prâna*: we shall see what it is as we go on. The *prâna* and the *âkâsa* exist as long as creation lasts. They combine and recombine and form all gross manifestations until at the end of the cycle all these subside and go back to the unmanifested form of *âkâsa* and *prâna.* There is in the Rig Veda, the oldest scriptures in existence, a beautiful passage describing creation, which is most poetical—"When there was neither ought nor nought, when darkness was rolling over darkness, what existed ?" and the answer is given, "It (the Eternal One) then existed without motion."* *Prâna*

* **Rig Veda—Mandal 10th, 129 Shukta.**

and *âkâsa* were latent in that Eternal One, but there was no phenomenal manifestation. This state is called *Avyaktam*, which literally means "without vibration," or unmanifested. At the beginning of a new cycle of evolution, this *avyaktam* begins to vibrate and blow after blow is given by *prâna* to the *âkâsa* causing condensation and gradually, through the forces of attraction and repulsion, atoms are formed. These in turn condense into molecules and finally into the different gross elements of which every object in nature is composed.

We generally find these things very curiously translated; people do not go to the ancient philosophers or to their commentators for their translation and have not learning enough to understand for themselves. They translate the elements as "air," "fire," and so on. If they would go to the commentators they would find that they do not mean anything of the sort. The *âkâsa*, by the repeated blows of *prâna*, produces *vâyu* or the vibratory state of the *âkâsa*, which in turn produces gaseous matter. The vibrations growing more and more rapid generate heat, which in Sanskrit is called *tejas*. Gradually it is cooled off and the gaseous substance becomes liquid, *Âpa* and finally solid, *prithivi*. We have first *âkâsa* vibrating, then comes heat, then it becomes liquified, and when still more condensed it appears as solid matter. It goes back to the unmanifested condition in exactly the reverse way. The solids will be converted into liquid and the liquid into a mass of heat, that will slowly go back into the gaseous state, then disintegradation of atoms will begin and finally the equilibrium of all forces will be reached, when vibration will stop and thus the cycle of evolution which in Sanskrit is called *Kalpa* will be at an end. We know from modern astronomy that this earth and sun of ours are undergoing the same transitions, this solid earth will melt down and become liquid once more, and will eventually go back to the gaseous state.

Prâna cannot work alone without the help of *âkâsa*. All that we know of it is motion or vibration. Every movement that we see is a modification of this *prâna*, and everything that we know in the form of matter, either as form or as resistance, is a modification of this *âkâsa*. The *prâna* cannot exist alone, or act without a medium, and in every state of it, whether as pure *prâna*, or when it changes into other forces of nature, as gravitation or centrifugal attraction, it can never be separate from *âkâsa*. You have never seen force without matter or matter without force; what we call force and matter being simply the gross manifestations of the two and these when superfine, the old philosophers have called *prâna* and *âkâsâ*. *Prâna* you can call in

English, life, or vital energy, but you must not restrict it to the life of man, nor should you identify it with the spirit, *Âtman*. Thus creation is a product of *prâna* and *âkâsa* and is without beginning and end; it cannot have either, for it is eternally going on.

The next question that comes is rather a fine one. Some European philosophers have asserted that this world exists because "I" exist, and if "I" do not exist, the world will not exist. Sometimes it is expressed thus—if all the people in the world were to die, and there were no more human beings, and no animals with powers of perception and intelligence, all manifestations would disappear. It seems paradoxical, but gradually we shall see clearly that this can be proved. But these European philosophers do not know the psychology of it, although they know the principle; they have only a glimpse of it.

First we shall consider another proposition of these old psychologists which is rather startling, that the grossest elements are the *bhutas*, but that all gross things are the results of fine ones. Everything that is gross is composed of a combination of fine things, so the *bhutas* must be composed of certain fine particles, called in Sanskrit the *tanmâtras*. I smell a flower; in doing so, something must have come in contact with my nose. The flower is there, I do not see it move towards me; but without something coming in contact with my nose how can I have the smell? That which comes from the flower and into contact with my nose are the *tanmâtras*, fine molecules of that flower, so fine that no diminution will be perceived in the flower even if we all smell it the whole day. So with heat, light, sight, and everything. These *tanmâtras* can again be subdivided into atoms. Different philosophers have different theories about the dimensions of atoms but we know these are only theories, so we leave them out of discussion. Sufficient for us that everything gross is composed of things that are very, very minute. We first get the gross elements, which we feel externally, and composing them are the fine elements, which our organs touch, which come in contact with the nerves of the nose, eyes and ears. The ethereal wave which touches my eyes, I cannot see, yet I know it must come in contact with my optic nerve before I can see the light. So with hearing, we can never see the particles that come in contact with our ears, but we know that they must be there. What is the cause of these *tanmâtras?* A very startling and curious answer is given by our psychologists,—self-consciousness. That is the cause of these fine materials, and the cause of the organs. What are these organs? Here is the eye, but the eye does not see. If the eyes did see, when a man is dead, and his eyes are still perfect, they would still be able to see. There is some change somewhere ; something has gone out of the man, and that something, which really sees and of which the eye is but the instrument, is called the organ. So this nose is an instrument, and there is an organ corresponding to it. Modern physiology can tell you what that is, a nerve centre in the brain. The eyes, ears, etc., are simply the external instruments. Thus the organs, *Indriyas*, as they are called in Sanskrit, are the real seats of perception.

What is the use of having one organ for the nose, and one for the eyes, and so on ? Why will not one serve the purpose ? To make it clear to you,—I am talking, and you are listening, and you do not see what is going on around you because the mind has attached itself to the organ of hearing, and has detached itself from the sight-organ. If there were only one organ, the mind would see and hear and smell at the same time, and it would be impossible for it not to do all three at the same time. Therefore it is necessary that there should be separate organs for all these centres. This has been borne out by modern physiology. It is certainly possible for us to see and hear at the same time, but that is because the mind attaches itself partially to both centres, which are the organs. What are the instruments ? We see that these are external and made of the gross materials. Here they are,—eyes, nose, and ears, etc. Of what are the organs made ? They are made of finer materials and are internal things because they are the centres. Just as this body is composed of gross material for transforming *prâna* into different gross forces, so these finer organs behind, are composed of finer materials, for the manufacture of *prâna* into the finer forces of perception. All these organs or *indriyas* combined, plus the internal instrument or *antahkarana*, are called the finer body of man,—the *linga* (or *sûkshma*) *sarira*.

It has a real form, because everything material must have a form. Behind the *indriyas* is the *manas*, the *chitta* in *vritti*, what might be called the vibratory or the unsettled state of the mind. If you throw a stone into a calm lake, first there will be vibration, and then resistance. For a moment the water will vibrate and then it will react on the stone. So, when any impression comes on the *chitta*, or "mind stuff," it vibrates a little. This state of the mind is called the *manas*. Then comes the reaction, the will.* There is another thing behind this will which accompanies all the acts of the mind, which is

* Sanskrit—*Buddhi*, the determining or decisive faculty of the mind

called egoism, the *ahamkâra*, the self-consciousness, which says "I am," and behind that is what is called *Mahat*,* the intelligence, the highest form of nature's existence. Behind the intellect is the true Self of man, the *Purusha*, the pure, the perfect, who is alone the seer, and for whom is all this change. The *Purusha* is looking on at all these changes. He himself is never impure; but by implication, by what the Vedantists call *adhyâsam*, or reflection, he appears to be so—as when a red flower is held before a piece of crystal, the crystal will look red or a blue flower and the crystal will look blue and yet the crystal itself is colorless. There are many *Purushas* or Selves; each pure and perfect, and it is all these various divisions of gross matter and fine matter that are imposing on Them and making Them appear variously colored. Why is *Prakriti* doing all this? *Prakriti* is

* Literally means great. Sometimes called *Buddhi*.

undergoing all these changes for the enjoyment and the benefit of the Self, so that it will realise its free nature. This immense book which we call the universe is stretched before man so that he may read, and come out,as an omniscient and omnipotent being. I must here tell you that some of our best psychologists do not believe in a personal God in the sense in which you believe in Him. The father of all psychologists, Kapila,denies the existence of God as Creator. His idea is that a personal God is quite unnecessary ; *Prakriti* is sufficient to work out all that is good. He repudiated the so-called "Design" theory of the universe. A more childish theory has never been advanced. But he admits a peculiar kind of God. He says we are all struggling to get free, and when man becomes free he can, as it were, melt away into *Prakriti* for the time being, to come out at the beginning of the next cycle an omniscient and omnipotent being and be its ruler. In that sense he can be called God. Thus you and I and the humblest beings will be gods in different cycles. Kapila says there can be such a temporal God, but an eternal God, eternally omnipotent and eternally ruler of the universe, there can never be. If there were such a God, there would be this difficulty—he must either be bound or free. A God who is perfectly free would not create; there would be no necessity. If he were bound, he would not create because he could not, he would be weak himself. So, in either case, there cannot be an omnipotent or omniscient eternal ruler. So wherever the word God is mentioned in our Scriptures, the Vedas, Kapila says it means those perfected souls who have become free. The *Sânkhya* system does not believe in the unity of all souls. Vedânta believes that all individual souls are united in one cosmic Being called

Brahman, but Kapila, the founder of the *Sânkhya*, was dualistic. His analysis of the universe so far as it goes is really marvellous. He was the father of Hindu evolutionists, and all the later philosophical systems are simply outcomes of his thought.

According to this system all souls will regain their freedom and their natural rights, which are omnipotence and omniscience. Here the question may be asked, whence is this bondage of the souls? The *Sânkhya* says it is without beginning: but if it be without beginning it must also be without end and we shall never be free. Kapila explains that this "without beginning" means not in a constant line. *Prakriti* is without beginning and without end, but not in the same sense as is the soul or *Purusha* because *Prakriti* has no individuality, just as a river flowing by us is every moment getting a fresh body of water, and the sum total of all these bodies of water is the river and yet the river is not a constant quantity. Similarly everything in *Prakriti* is constantly changing, but the soul never changes. Therefore as *Prakriti* is always changing, it is possible for the soul to come out of its bondage. One theory of the *Sânkhya* is peculiar to this psychology. The whole of the universe is built upon the same plan as one single man, or one little being ; so, just as I have a mind, there is also a cosmic mind. When this macrocosm evolves there must be first intelligence, then egoism, then the *tanmâtras* and the organs, and then the gross elements. The whole universe according to Kapila is one body, all that we see are the grosser bodies, and behind these are the finer bodies, and behind them, a universal egoism, and behind that a universal Intelligence ; but all these are in *Prakriti*, all these are manifestations of *Prakriti* not outside of it. Each one of us is a part of that cosmic consciousness. There is a sum-total of intelligence out of which we draw what we require, so there is a sum-total of mental force in the universe out of which we are drawing eternally, but the seed for the body must come from the parents. The theory includes heredity and reincarnation too. The material is given to the soul out of which to manufacture a body, but that material is given by hereditary transmission from the parents.

We come now to the proposition that in this process there is an involution and an evolution. All is evolved out of that indiscreet *Prakriti*; and then is involved again and becomes *Avyaktam*. It is impossible, according to the *Sânkhyas*, for any material thing to exist, which has not as its material some portion of consciousness. Consciousness is the material out of which all manifestation is made. The elucidation of this comes in our next lecture, but I will show

how it can be proved. I do not know this table as it is, but it makes an impression; it comes to the eyes, then to the *indriyas*, and then to the mind; the mind then reacts, and that reaction is what I call the table. It is just the same as throwing a stone into a lake; the lake throws a wave against the stone; this wave is what we know. The waves coming out are all we know. In the same way the fashion of this wall is in my mind; what is external nobody knows; when I want to know it, it has to become that material which I furnish; I, with my own mind, have furnished the material for my eyes, and the something which is outside is only the occasion, the suggestion, and upon that suggestion I project my mind, and it takes the form of what I see. The question is, how do we all see the same things? Because we all have a part of this cosmic mind. Those who have mind will see the thing, and those who have not will not see it. This goes to show that since this universe has existed there has never been a want of mind, of that one cosmic mind. Every human being, every animal, is also furnished out of that cosmic mind, because it is always present and furnishing material for their formation.

II

PRAKRITI AND PURUSHA

WE will take up the categories we have been discussing and come to the particulars. If we remember we started with *Prakriti*. This has been called by the *Sânkhya* philosophers indiscrete or inseparate, and defined as perfect balance of the materials in it; and it naturally follows that in perfect balance there cannot be any motion. All that we see, feel, and hear is simply a compound of motion and matter. In the primal state, before this manifestation, where there was no motion, perfect balance, this *Prakriti* was indestructible, because decomposition comes only with limitation. Again, according to the *Sânkhya*, atoms are not the primal state. This universe does not come out of atoms, they may be the secondary, or tertiary state. The original matter may compound into atoms, which in turn compound into greater and greater things, and as far as modern investigations go, they rather point towards that. For instance, in the modern theory of ether, if you say ether is also atomic, that will not solve the proposition at all. To make it clearer, say that air is composed of atoms ; and we know that ether is everywhere, interpenetrating, omnipresent, and that atoms are floating, as it were, in ether. If ether again be composed of atoms, there will still be some space between two atoms of ether. What fills up that ? And again there will be another space between the atoms of that which fills up this space. If you propose that there is another ether still finer you must still have something to fill that space, and so it will be *regressus in infinitum*, what the *Sânkhya* philosophers call *anavasthâ*,–never reaching a final conclusion. So the atomic theory cannot be final. According to the *Sânkhyas* this *Prakriti* is omnipresent, one omnipresent mass of matter in which are the causes of everything that exists. What is meant by cause? Cause is the more subtle state of the manifested state, the unmanifested state of that which becomes manifested. What do you mean by destruction? It is reverting to the cause, —the materials out of which a body is composed go back into their original state. Beyond this idea of destruction, any idea such as annihilation, is on the face of it absurd. According to modern physical sciences, it can be demonstrated that all destruction means that which Kapila called ages ago "reverting to the causal state." Going back to the finer form is all that is meant by destruction. You know how it can be demonstrated in a laboratory that matter is indestructible. Those of you who have studied chemistry will know that if you place a candle and a caustic pencil inside a glass tube and let the candle burn away, then take the caustic pencil out of the tube and weigh it, you will find that the pencil will weigh exactly its previous weight, plus the weight of the candle,—the candle became finer and finer, and went on to the caustic. So that in this present stage of our knowledge, if any man claims that anything becomes annihilated, he is only making himself absurd. It is only uneducated people who would advance such a proposition, and it is curious that modern knowledge coincides with what those old philosophers taught. The ancients proceeded in their inquiry by taking up mind as the basis ; they analyzed the mental part of this universe and came to certain conclusions, while modern science is analyzing the physical part, and it also has come to the same conclusions. Both analyses have led to the same truth.

You must remember that the first manifestation of this *Prakriti* in the cosmos is what the *Sânkhyas* called *Mahat*. We may call it universal intelligence—the great principle; that is the literal meaning. The first manifestation of *Prakriti* is this intelligence; I would not translate it by self-consciousness, because that would be wrong. Consciousness is only a part of this intelligence, which is universal. It covers all the grounds of consciousness, sub-consciousness and super-consciousness. In nature, for instance, certain changes are going on before your eyes which you see and understand, but there are other changes so much finer that no human perception can catch them. They are from the same cause, the same *Mahat* is making these changes. There are other changes, beyond the reach of our mind or reasoning, all these series of changes are in this *Mahat*. You will understand it better when I come to the individual. Out of this *Mahat* comes the universal egoism, and these are both material. There is no difference between matter and mind save in degree. It is the same substance in finer or grosser form; one changes into the other, and this will exactly coincide with the modern physiological research, and will save you from a great deal of fighting and struggling if you believe it than that you have a mind separate from the brain, and all such impossible things. This substance called *Mahat* changes into the material called egoism, the fine state of matter, and that egoism changes into two varieties. In one variety it changes into the organs. Organs are of two kinds—organs of sensation and organs of reaction.* They are not the eyes or nose, but something finer; what you call brain centres, and nerve

* Organs of sensation—The nerve centres by which we see, hear, smell, taste and touch. Organs of reaction—The nerve centres regulating hands, feet, voice, excretion and procreation.

centres. This egoism becomes changed, and out of this material are manufactured these centres and these nerves. Out of the same substance, the egoism, is manufactured another fine form, the *tanmâtras*, fine particles of matter, those for instance which strike your nose and cause you to smell. You cannot perceive these fine particles, you can only know that they are there. The *tanmâtras* are manufactured out of the egoism, and out of the *tanmâtras*, or subtle matter, is manufactured the gross matter, air, water, earth, and all the things that we see and feel. I want to impress this on your mind. It is very hard to grasp it, because, in Western countries, the ideas are so queer about mind and matter. It is hard to take these impressions out of our brains. I myself had tremendous difficulty, being educated in Western philosophy in my childhood.

These are all cosmic things. Think of

this universal extension of matter, unbroken, one substance, undifferentiated, which is the first state of everything, and which begins to change just as milk becomes curd, and that it is changed into another substance called *Mahat*, which in one state manifests as intelligence and in another state as egoism. It is the same substance, only changed into the grosser matter called egoism. Thus is the whole universe itself built, as it were, layer after layer; first undifferentiated *Prakriti* (*Avyaktam*), and that changes into universal intelligence (*Mahat*), and that again is changed into universal egoism (*Ahamkâra*), and that changes into universal sensible matter. That matter changes into universal sense-organs, again changes into universal fine particles, and these in turn combine and become this gross universe. This is the cosmic plan, according to the *Sânkhyas*, and what is in the cosmos or macrocosm, must be in the individual or microcosm.

Take an individual man. He has first a part of undifferentiated nature in him, and that material nature in him becomes changed into *mahat*, a small particle of the universal intelligence, and that small particle of the universal intelligence in him becomes changed into egoism—a particle of the universal egoism. This egoism in turn becomes changed into the sense-organs, and the *tanmâtras*, and out of the latter combining he manufactures his world, his body. I want this to be clear, because it is the first stepping stone to Vedânta, and it is absolutely necessary for you to know, because this is the basis of the different systems of philosophy of the whole world. There is no philosophy in the world that is not indebted to Kapila, the founder of this *Sânkhya* system. Pythagoras came to India and studied this philosophy and carried some of these ideas to the Greeks. Later it formed the Alexandrian school, and still later formed the basis of Gnostic philosophy. Thus it became divided into two parts; one went to Europe and Alexandria, and the other remained in India, and became the basis of all Hindu philosophy, for out of it the system of Vyâsa was developed. This was the first rational system that the world saw, this system of Kapila. Every metaphysician in the world must pay homage to him. I want to impress on your mind that as the great father of philosophy, we are bound to listen to him, and respect what he said. This wonderful man, most ancient of philosophers, is mentioned even in the Vedas. How wonderful his perceptions were! If there is any proof required of the power of the Yogis to perceive things beyond the range of the ordinary senses, such men are the proofs. How could they perceive them? They had no microscopes, or telescopes. How fine their perception was, how perfect their analysis and how wonderful!

To revert again to the microcosm, man. As we have seen, he is built on exactly the same plan. First the nature is "indiscrete" or perfectly balanced, then it becomes disturbed, and action sets in and the first change produced by that action is what is called *mahat*,—intelligence. Now you see this intelligence in man is just a particle of the cosmic intelligence,—the *Mahat*. Out of it comes self-consciousness, and from this the sensory and the motor nerves, and the finer particles out of which the gross body is manufactured. I will here remark that there is one difference between Schopenhauer and Vedânta. Schopenhauer says that desire, or will, is the cause of everything. It is the will to exist that makes us manifest, but the Advaitists deny this. They say it is the intelligence. There cannot be a single particle of will which is not a reaction. So many things are beyond will. It is only a manufactured something out of the ego, and the ego is a a product of something still higher, the intelligence, and that is a modification of "indiscrete" Nature, or *Prakriti.*

It is very important to understand this *mahat* in man,—the intelligence. This intelligence itself is modified into what we call egoism, and this intelligence is the cause of all these changes which result in producing the body. This covers all the grounds of sub-consciousness, consciousness and super-consciousness. What are these three states ? The sub-conscious state is what we find in animals, and call instinct. This is nearly infallible, but very limited. Instinct almost never fails. An animal instinctively knows a poisonous herb from an edible one, but its instinct is limited to one or two things; it works like a machine. Then comes the higher state of knowlege, which is fallible, makes mistakes often, but has a larger scope, although it is slow, and this you call reason. It is much larger than instinct, but there are more dangers of mistake in reasoning than in instinct. There is a still higher state of the mind, the super-conscious, which belongs only to the Yogis, men who have cultivated it. This is as infallible as instinct, and still more unlimited than reason. It is the highest state. We must remember that as in man this *mahat* is the real cause of all that which is manifesting itself in various ways, covering the whole ground of his sub-conscious, conscious and super-conscious states—the three states in which knowledge exists—so in the Cosmos, this universal Intelligence, *Mahat*, exists as instinct, as reason, and as super-reason.

Now comes a delicate question, which is

always being asked. If a perfect God created the universe, why is there imperfection in it ? What we call the universe is what we see, and that is only this little plane of consciousness or reason, and beyond that we do not see at all. Now the very question is an impossible one. If I take up only a bit out of a mass and look at it, it seems to be imperfect. Naturally. The universe seems imperfect because we make it so. How ? What is reason ? What is knowledge ? Knowledge is finding associations. You go into the street and see a man, and know it is a man. You have seen many men, and each one has made an impression on your mind, and when you now see this man, you calmly refer to your store of impressions, see many pictures of men there, and you put this new one with the rest, pigeon-hole it and are satisfied. When a new impression comes and it has associations in your mind, you are satisfied, and this state of association is called knowledge. Knowledge is, therefore, pigeon-holing one experience with the already existing fund of experience, and this is one of the great proofs that you cannot have any knowledge until you have already a fund in existence. If you are without experience, or if, as some European philosophers think, the mind is a *tabula rasa*, it cannot get any knowledge, because the very fact of knowledge is the recognition of the new by comparison with already existing impressions. There must be a store ready to which to refer a new impression. Suppose a child is born into this world without such a fund, it would be impossible for him to get any knowledge. Therefore the child must have been in a state in which he had a fund, and so knowledge is eternally going on. Show me any way of getting out of this. It is mathematical experience. This is very much like the Spencerian and some other western philosophies. They have seen so far that there cannot be any knowledge without a fund of past knowledge and that therefore the child is born with knowledge. They have found out the truth that the cause enters into the effect, that it comes in a subtle form in order to be developed. But these philosophers say that these impressions with which the child comes, are not from the child's own past, but were in his forefathers' and have come to the child by hereditary transmission. Very soon they are going to find this theory untenable, and some of them are even now giving hard blows to the idea of heredity. Heredity is very good, but incomplete. It only explains the physical side. How would you explain the influence of environment in accordance with it? Many causes produce an effect and environment is one of them. On the other hand the Hindu philosophers say that we make our own environment, because as our past was, so we find our present. In other words, we are what we are here and now, because of what we were in the past.

You understand now what is meant by knowledge. Knowledge is pigeon-holing a new impression with old impressions—recognizing a new impression. What is meant by recognition? Finding its association with similar impressions that we already have. Nothing further is meant by knowledge. If that be the case, it must be that we have to see the whole series of similars in the process. Is it not? Suppose you are to know a pebble; to find its association, you will have to see the whole series of pebbles similar to it. But with the universe we cannot do that, because in our reasoning we see only one perception of it and can neither see on this side nor on that side of it and refer it to its association. Therefore the universe seems unintelligible, because knowledge and reason are always finding associations. This bit of the universe cut off by our consciousness is a startling new thing, and we are not able to find its associations. Therefore we are struggling with it, and we think it is so horrible, so wicked, and bad—sometimes we think it is good, but generally imperfect. The universe will be known only when we find its associations. We shall recognize them when we go beyond the universe and our little self-consciousness, and then alone the universe will stand explained. Until we do that all our fruitless striving will never explain it—because knowledge is the finding of similars, and this conscious plane gives us only a partial view of the universe. So with our idea of the universal *Mahat*, or what in our ordinary everyday language we call God. All that we have of the idea of God is only one perception, a partial view of Him and all the rest is cut off and covered by our human limitation. "I, the Universal, so great am I that even this universe is a part of me." * That is why we see God as imperfect, and we can never understand Him, because it is impossible. The only way to understand Him is to go beyond reason, beyond self-consciousness. "When thou goest beyond the heard and hearing, the thought and thinking, then alone wilt thou come to Truth." † "Go thou beyond the Scriptures, because they teach only up to *Prakriti*, up to the three qualities of which It is composed and out of which evolves the universe." ‡ When we go beyond them we find the harmony, not before.

---

* Bhagavad Gita X 42.

† Bhagavad Gita II. 52.

‡ Gita II. 45.

So far it is clear that this macrocosm and microcosm are built on exactly the same plan, and of this microcosm we know only one very small part. We know neither the sub-conscious, nor the super-conscious. We know only the conscious. If a man says "I am a sinner," he is foolish, because he does not know himself. He is the most ignorant of men about himself; one part of himself only he knows, because the fact of knowledge covers only one part of the "mind-ground" he is in. So with this universe; it is possible to know only one part through reasoning, but *Prakriti* comprises the whole of it, the sub-conscious, the conscious and the super-conscious, the individual *mahat* and the universal *Mahat* with all their subsequent modifications, and these lie beyond reason.

What makes *Prakriti* change? We have seen up to this point that everything in nature, *Prakriti* itself, is *jadâ* (insentient).

It is working under law; it is all compound and insentient. Mind, intelligence, and will, all are insentient. But they are all reflecting the sentiency, the *Chit* (Intelligence) of some Being who is beyond all this, and whom the Sânkhya philosophers call *Purusha*. This *Purusha* is the unwitting cause of all these changes in *Prakriti*—in the universe. That is to say, this *Purusha*, taking Him in the universal sense, is the God of the universe. It is claimed that the will of the Lord created the universe. This is very good as a common daily expression, but that is all. How could it be will? Will is the third or fourth manifestation out of *Prakriti*. Many things exist before it; and what created *them?* Will is a compound, and everything that is a compound is a production out of *Prakriti*. Will itself cannot create *Prakriti*. It is not a simple. So to say that the will of the Lord created the universe is illogical. In man will covers a little portion only of self-consciousness. It moves our brain, some say. If it did you could stop the action of the brain, but you cannot. It is not the will. Who moves the heart ? It is not the will ; because if it were you could stop it at your will. It is neither will that is working your body, nor the universe. But it is something of which will itself is one of the manifestations. This body is being moved by a power of which will is only a manifestation in one part. So in the universe there is will, but that is only one part of the universe. The whole of the universe is not guided by will, that is why we do not find the explanation of it in will. Suppose I take it for granted that the will is moving the body, and then begin to fret and fume. It is my fault, because I had no right to take it for granted that it was will. In the same way, if I take the universe and think it is will that moves it and then find that things do not coincide, it is my fault. This *Purusha* is not will, neither can it be intelligence, because intelligence itself is a compound. There cannot be any intelligence without some sort of matter. In man, this matter takes the form which we call brain. Wherever there is intelligence there must be matter in some form or other. Thus intelligence being a compound what then is this *Purusha?* It is neither intelligence nor *buddhi* (will), but yet it is the cause of both these ; it is His presence that sets them all vibrating and combining. *Purusha* may be likened to some of those substances which by their mere presence promote chemical reaction, as in the case of cyanide of potassium which is added when gold is being smelted. The cyanide of potassium remains separate and unaffected, but its presence is absolutely necessary to the success of the process. So with the *Purusha.*

It does not mix with *Prakriti* ; it is not Intelligence, or *Mahat*, or any one of its modifications but the Self, the Pure, the Perfect. "I am the Witness and through My witnessing, *Prakriti* is producing all that is sentient and all that is insentient."*

Whence then is this sentiency in *Prakriti* ? Its basis is in the *Purusha*, and it is the very nature of the *Purusha*. It is that which cannot be expressed or understood, but which is the material of all that we call knowledge. This *Purusha* is not consciousness, because consciousness is a compound, but whatever is radient and good in this consciousness belongs to It. Sentiency is in the *Purusha*, but the *Purusha* is not intelligent, not knowing, it is the very condition in which knowledge is possible. The *Chit* in the *Purusha*, plus *Prakriti*, is what is known to us as intelligence and consciousness. All the joy and

---

* Gita IX. 10.

happiness and light in the universe belongs to the *Purusha*, but it is a compound because it is that *Purusha* plus *Prakriti*. "Wherever there is any happiness, wherever there is any bliss, there is one spark of that immortality, which is *Purusha*."* This *Purusha* is the great attraction of the universe; untouched by, and unconnected with the universe, yet it attracts the whole universe. You see a man going after gold, because therein is a spark of the *Purusha*, even though he knows it not. When a man desires children, or a woman a husband, what is the attracting power? That spark of *Purusha* behind the child and the husband. It is there, behind everything only overlaid with matter. Nothing else can attract. "In this world of insentiency that *Purusha* alone is sentient."† This is the *Purusha* of the *Sânkhyas*. As such it

* Brihadâranyaka Upanishada IV. 3—32.

† Katha Upanishada V. 13.

necessarily follows that this *Purusha* must be omnipresent for that which is not omnipresent must be limited. All limitations are caused and that which is caused must have beginning and end. If the *Purusha* is limited it will die, will not be final, will not be free, but will have been caused. Therefore if not limited, it is omnipresent. According to Kapila there are many *Purushas*, not one. An infinite number of them, you are one, I am one, each is one ; an infinite number of circles, each one infinite, running through this universe. The *Purusha* is neither born nor dies. It is neither mind nor matter, and the reflex from it is all that we know. We are sure if it be omnipresent it knows neither death nor birth. *Prakriti* is casting her shadow upon it, the shadow of birth and death, but it is by its own nature eternal. So far we have found the theory of Kapila wonderful.

Next we will have to take up the proofs

against it. So far the analysis is perfect, the psychology cannot be controverted. There is no objection to it. We asked of Kapila the question : Who created *Prakriti* ? and his answer was that *Prakriti* is uncreate. He has also said that the *Purusha* is uncreate and omnipresent and that of these *Purushas* there is an infinite number. We shall have to controvert this last proposition, and find a better solution, and by so doing we shall come to the ground taken by Vedânta. Our first doubt will be how there can be these two infinites. Then our argument will be that it is not a perfect generalization, and that therefore we have not found a perfect solution. And then we shall see how the Vedantists find their way out of all these difficulties and reach a perfect solution. Yet all the glory really belongs to Kapila. It is very easy to give a finish to a building that is nearly complete.

III

SÂNKHYA AND ADVAITA

I WILL give you first a *resumé* of the *Sânkhya* philosophy, which we have been studying, because in this lecture we want to find where its defects are, and where Vedânta comes in to supplement these deficiencies. You must remember that according to the *Sânkhya* philosophy, *Prakriti* is causing all these manifestations which we call thought, intellect and reason, love, hatred, touch and taste ; that everything is from *Prakriti.* This *Prakriti* consists of three sorts of elements, one called *Sattva*, another *Rajas*, and the third *Tamas*. These are not qualities, but the materials out of which the whole universe is being evolved, and at the beginning of a cycle they remain in equilibrium. When creation comes this equilibrium is disturbed and

E

these elements begin to combine and re-combine, and manifest as the universe. The first manifestation of these is what the *Sânkhya* calls the *Mahat* (universal Intelligence), and out of that comes consciousness. And out of consciousness is evolved *Manas* (universal Mind). Out of this consciousness are also evolved the organs of perception and action and the *tanmâtras*,—sound particles, touch particles, taste particles, and so forth. All fine particles are evolved from this consciousness, and out of these fine particles come the gross particles which we call matter. After the *tanmâtras* (those particles which cannot be seen, or measured) come the gross particles which we can feel and sense. The *chitta* ("mind-stuff") in its three-fold functions of intellect, consciousness and mind* is working and manufacturing the forces called *prânas*. These *prânas* have nothing to do with

* Sanskrit equivalent: *Buddhi*, *Ahamkâra* and *manas*.

breath, you must at once get rid of that idea. Breath is one effect of the Prana (universal Energy). By the *prânas* are meant the nervous forces that are governing and moving the whole body, and manifesting themselves as thought, and as the various functions of the body. The foremost and the most obvious manifestation of these *prânas* is the breathing motion. If it were caused by air, a dead man would breathe. The *prâna* acts upon the air, and not air upon it. These *prânas* are the vital forces which manipulate the whole body, and they in turn are manipulated by the mind and the *indriyas* (the two kinds of organs). So far so good. The psychology is very clear and most precise, and just think of the age of it, the oldest rational thought in the world ! Wherever there is any philosophy or rational system of thought, it owes something to Kapila. Wherever there is any attempt at psychology, there is some indebtedness to the great father of this thought, to this man, Kapila.

So far we see that this psychology is wonderful, but we shall have to differ with it on some points, as we go on. We find that the principal idea on which Kapila works is evolution. He makes one thing evolve out of another, because his very definition of causation is "the effect is the cause reproduced in another form," * and because the whole universe, so far as we see it, is progressive and evolving. This whole universe must have evolved out of some material, out of *Prakriti*. Therefore the *Prakriti* cannot be essentially different from its cause, only when it takes form it becomes limited. The material itself is without form. But according to Kapila, from undifferentiated nature or prakriti down to the last stage of differentiation, none of these is the same as *Purusha*, the "Enjoyer,"

* Sânkhya Philosophy I. 118.

or "Enlightener." Just as a lump of clay, so is a mass of mind, and the whole universe. By itself it has no light, but we find reason and intelligence in it, therefore there must be some Existence behind it, behind the whole of *Prakriti*, whose light is percolating through it and appearing as *Mahat* and consciousness and all these various things, and this Existence is what Kapila calls the *Purusha*,or *Âtman* and the Vedantist Self. According to Kapila, the *Purusha* is a *simple* factor, not a compound. It is immaterial, the only one that is immaterial, whereas all the various manifestations are material. The *Purusha* alone knows. Suppose I see a blackboard, first the external instruments will bring that sensation to the organ (to the *indriya* according to Kapila), from the organ it will go to the mind and make an impression ; the mind will cover it up with another factor,—consciousness, and will present it to the *mahat* (intelligence), but *mahat* cannot act; it is the *Purusha* behind that acts. These are all its servants, bringing the sensation to It, and It gives the orders, and the *mahat* reacts. The *Purusha* is the Enjoyer, the Perceiver, the real One, the King on his throne, the Self of man, and It is immaterial. Because It is immaterial, it necessarily follows that It must be infinite, It cannot have any limitation whatever. So each one of these *purushas* is omnipresent, each is all-pervading, but can act only through fine and gross manifestations of matter. The mind, the self-consciousness, the organs and the vital forces compose what is called the fine body, or what in Christian philosophy is called the "spiritual body" of man. It is this body that comes to reward or punishment, that goes to the different heavens; that incarnates and reincarnates; because we see from the very beginning that the going and coming of the soul (*Purusha*) is impossible. Motion means going and coming, and that which goes from one place to another cannot be omnipresent. It is this *linga-sarira* (subtle body) which comes and goes. Thus far we see from Kapila's psychology that the soul is infinite, and that the soul is the only principle that is not an evolution of *Prakriti*. It is the only one that is outside of *Prakriti* but It has apparently become bound by *Prakriti*. *Prakriti* is surrounding the *Purusha* and so It has identified Itself with *Prakriti*. It thinks "I am the *linga-sarira*," It thinks "I am the gross matter, the gross body," and as such is enjoying pleasure and pain; but these do not really belong to the soul, they belong to this *linga-sarira*, and to the gross body. When certain nerves are hurt we feel pain. We recognize that immediately. If the nerves in our fingers were dead we could cut the fingers and not feel it. So pleasure and pain belong to the nerve-centres. Suppose my organ of sight is destroyed, I do not feel pleasure or pain from color, although my eyes are there. So it is obvious that pleasure and pain do not belong to the soul. They belong to the mind and the body.

The soul has neither pleasure nor pain; it is the Witness of everything, the eternal Witness of things that are going on, but it takes no fruits from any work. "As the sun is the cause of sight in every eye, yet is not itself affected by the defects in any eye such is the *Purusha.*"* "As a piece of crystal appears red when red flowers are placed before it, so this *Purusha* appears to be affected by pleasure or pain from the reflection cast upon It by Nature, but It remains ever unchanged."† The nearest way to describe Its state is that which

* Katha Upanishada—Chapter II. 2—11.

† Sânkhya Suttra. II. 35.

we feel during meditation. This meditative state is that in which you approach nearest to the *Purusha*. Thus we see why the meditative state is always called the highest state by the *Yogi*, for to feel one's self as one with the *Purusha* is neither a passive nor an active state, but the meditative state. This is the *Sânkhya* philosophy.

Next, the *Sânkhyas* say that this manifestation of *Prakriti* is for the Soul, that all the combinations of the materials of It are for something outside of It. So these combinations which we call nature, these constant changes within and arround are going on for the enjoyment of the Soul, for Its liberation, that It may gain all this experience from the lowest to the highest: and when It has gained it, the Soul finds that it never was in *Prakriti* but was entirely separate, and It finds that It is indestructible, that It neither goes nor comes, that going to heaven and being born again belong to *Prakriti* and not to Itself. So the soul becomes free. Thus all *Prakriti* is working for the enjoyment and experience of the Soul and It is getting this experience in order to reach the goal, and that goal is freedom. These Souls are many, according to the *Sânkhya* philosophy. There is an infinite number of them. And the other conclusion is that there is no God, no Creator of the universe. *Prakriti* herself being sufficient to produce all these forms, God is not necessary, say the *Sânkhyas.*

Now we shall have to contest these three positions of the *Sânkhyas.* First that intelligence or anything of that sort does not belong to the Soul, but that it belongs entirely to *Prakriti*, the Soul being simply qualitiless, colorless. The second point is that there is no God, and Vedânta will show that without a God there cannot be any explanation whatever. Thirdly, we shall have to contend that there cannot be many Souls, that there cannot be an infinite number of them, that there is only One Soul in the universe, and that One is appearing as many.

We will take the first proposition, that intelligence and reason belong entirely to *Prakriti*, and not to the Soul. The Vedânta says that the Soul is in its essence unlimited or absolute Existence-Knowledge-Bliss ; but we agree with the *Sânkhyas* that, that which they call intelligence is a compound. For instance, let us look at our perceptions. We remember that the *chitta* (or the "mind-stuff") is what is combining all these things, and upon which all these impressions are made,. and from which reactions come. Suppose there is something outside. I see the blackboard. How does the knowledge of it come ? The blackboard itself is unknown, I can never know it. It is what the German philosophers call the "thing in itself." That blackboard, that "X," is acting on my mind, and the *chitta* reacts. The *chitta* is like a lake: If you throw a stone upon a lake, as soon as the stone strikes it, a reactionary wave comes towards the stone. This wave is what you really see. And this wave is not like the stone at all, it is a wave. So that blackboard, "X," is the stone which strikes the mind and the mind throws up a wave towards that object which strikes it, and this wave which is thrown towards it is what we call the blackboard. I see you. You as you really are is unknown and unknowable. You are "X" and you act upon my mind, and the mind throws a wave towards the point from which the action came, and that wave is what I call Mr. or Mrs. So-and-So.

There are two elements in this, one from inside and the other from outside, and the combination of these two, "X" plus mind, is our external universe. All knowledge is by reaction. In the case of a whale it has been determined by calculation how long after its tail is struck, its mind reacts upon the tail and the tail feels the pain. Take the case of the pearl oyster, in which the pearl is formed by the oyster throwing its own juice around the grain of sand that enters the shell and irritates him. There are two things which cause the pearl. First the oyster's own juice, and second the blow from outside. So is my knowledge of this table, "X" plus my mind. The very attempt to know it will be made by the mind; therefore the mind will give some of its own substance to enable it to understand, and when we understand it, it has become a compound thing,—"X" plus the mind. Similarly in internal perception; when we want to know ourselves. The real Self, which is within us, is also unknown and unknowable. Let us call it "Y." When I want to know myself as Mr. So-and-So the "Y" has to appear as "Y" plus the mind. That "Y" strikes a blow on the mind, when I want to know myself and the mind must throw a blow upon the "Y" also. So our knowledge of the whole world is "X" plus mind (the external world), and "Y" plus mind (the internal world). We shall see later how the Advaitist idea can be demonstrated mathematically.

"X" and "Y" are simply the algebraic unknown quantities. We have seen that all knowledge is a combination, and so is this knowledge of the world, or the universe, a combination, and so is intelligence similarly a combination. If it is internal intelligence or mental experience it is "Y" plus the mind, if an external intelligence or experience of an object, it is "X" plus the mind. All internal knowledge is a combination of "Y" plus the mind and all knowledge of external matter is a combination of "X" plus the mind. We first take the internal group. The intelligence which we see in nature cannot be wholly in nature, because intelligence itself is a compound of "Y" plus the mind and "Y" comes from the Self. So the intelligence that we know is a compound of the power of the light of the soul plus nature. Similarly, the existence which we know must be a compound of "X" plus the mind. We find therefore that in these three factors, I exist, I know and I am blessed, (the idea that I have no want, which comes from time to time) is the central idea, the grand basic idea of our life, and in proportion as this centre or basis becomes limited, and becomes a compound, we think it happiness or misery. These factors manifest as existence phenomenal, knowledge phenomenal, and love phenomenal. Every man exists, and every man must know, and every man is made for bliss. He cannot help it. So through all existence. Animals and plants, from the lowest to the highest existence, all must love. You may not call *it love*; *but they must* all *exist, must* all know and must all love. So this existence which we know is a compound of "X" and the mind, and knowledge, is a compound of that "Y" inside plus mind, and that love also is a compound of that "Y" and mind. Therefore these three factors which come from inside and are combining themselves with the external things to manufacture phenomenal existence, knowledge and love, are called by the Vedantists "Existence Absolute, Knowledge Absolute, Bliss Absolute."

That Absolute Existence which is limitless, which is unmixed, uncombined, which knows no change, is the free Soul, and that Real Existence, when it gets *mixed* up, muddled up, as it were, with the elements of nature is what we call human existence. It becomes limited and manifests as plant life, animal life, human life, just as infinite space is apparently limited by the walls of this room, or by any other enclosure. That Knowledge Absolute means not the knowledge we know, not intelligence, not reason, not instinct, but that which when it becomes manifested we call by these names. When that Knowledge Absolute becomes limited we call it intuition, and when it becomes still more limited we call it reason, instinct, etc. That Knowledge Absolute is *Vijnâna*. The nearest translation of it is "all-knowingness." There is no combination in it. It is the nature of the soul. That Bliss Absolute when it becomes limited we call love, attraction for the gross body, or the fine bodies, or for ideas. These are but distorted manifestations of this blessedness which is not a quality of the soul, but the essence, the inherent nature of the soul. Absolute Existence, Absolute Knowledge, and Absolute Blessedness are not qualities of the soul, but its essence; there is no difference between them and the soul. And the three are one; we see the one thing in three different lights. They are beyond all knowledge and by their reflection *Prakriti* appears to be intelligent.

It is that eternal Knowledge Absolute of the Self percolating through the mind of man that becomes our reason and intelligence. It varies according to the medium through which it is shining. There is no difference as soul between me and the lowest animal, only his brain is a poorer medium through which the knowledge shines, and we call it instinct. In man the brain is much finer, so the manifestation is much clearer, and in the highest man it has become entirely clear, like a piece of glass. So with existence; this existence which we know, this limited bit of existence is simply a reflection of that Existence Absolute which is the nature of the soul. So with bliss ; that which we call love or attraction is but the reflection of the eternal blessedness of the Self, because with these manifestations come limitations, but the unmanifested, the natural, essential existence of the soul is unlimited, to that blessedness there can be no limit. But in human love there are limitations. I may love you one day, I may cease to love you the next. My love increases one day, decreases the next, because it is only a limited manifestation. The first thing therefore that we find against Kapila is that he conceives the soul to be a mere qualitiless, colorless, inactive something. Vedânta teaches that it is the essence of all Existence, Knowledge, and Bliss ; infinitely higher than all knowledge that we know, infinitely more blessed than any human love that we can think of, infinitely existing. The soul never dies. Death and birth are simply unthinkable in connection with the Self, because it is Existence Absolute.

The second point where we will contend with Kapila is with regard to his idea of God. Just as this series of limited manifestations of *Prakriti*, beginning with the individual intellect and ending with the individual body, requires the Self behind as the ruler and governor on the throne, so in the Cosmos, we must enquire what the universal Intelligence, the universal Mind, the universal fine and gross materials have as their ruler and governor? How will that series become complete without one universal Self behind it as its ruler and governor? If we deny that there is a universal governor, we must deny there is a soul behind the lesser series, because the whole universe is a repetition of the same plan. When we know one lump of clay we know the nature of all clay. If we can analyze one human being, we shall have analyzed the whole universe, because it is all built on the same plan. Therefore if it be true that behind this individual series there stands one who is beyond all nature, who is not composed of materials, the *purusha*, the very same logic will apply to this universe, and this universe too will require such a Soul. The Universal Soul which is behind the modifications of *Prakriti* is called by Vedânta *Isvara*, the Supreme Ruler, God.

Now comes the more difficult point to fight. There can be but one Soul. To begin with, we can give the *Sânkhyas* a good blow by taking up their theories and proving that each soul must be omnipresent, because it is not composed of anything. Everything that is limited must be limited by something else. Here is the existence of the table. Its existence is circumscribed by many things, and we find that every limitation presupposes some limiting thing. If we think of space, we have to think of it as a little circle, but beyond that is more space. We cannot imagine a limited space in any other way. It can only be understood and perceived through the infinite. To perceive the finite, in every case we must apprehend the infinite ; both stand or fall together. When you think of time, you have also to think of time beyond any particular period of time. The latter is limited time and the larger is unlimited time. Wherever you endeavor to perceive the finite, you will find it impossible to separate it from the infinite. If this be the case, we shall prove thereby that this Self must be infinite, omnipresent. Then comes a fine question. Can the omnipresent, the infinite be two? Suppose there are two infinites, one will limit the other. Suppose there are two infinites,—A and B; the infinite "A" limits the infinite "B," because the infinite " B " you can say is not the infinite "A, " and the infinite " A " it can be said is not the infinite " B. " Therefore there can be but one infinite. Secondly, the infinite cannot be divided. Infinity divided into any number of parts must still be infinity, for it cannot be separated from itself. Suppose there is an infinite ocean of water, could you take up one drop from there? If you could, that ocean would no longer be infinite, that drop would limit it. The infinite cannot be divided by any means.

But there are stronger proofs that the Self is One. Not only so, but that the whole universe is one. We will once more take up our "X" and "Y". We have shown how what we call the external world is "X plus mind," and the internal world "Y plus mind." "X" and "Y" are both unknown quantities, unknown and unknowable. What is the mind? The mind is "time, space and causation." These form the very essence of the mind. You can never think without time, you can never conceive of anything without space, and you can never imagine anything without causation. These three are the forms in which both "X" and "Y" are caught, and become limited by the mind. Beyond them there is nothing else in the constitution of the mind. Take off these three forms which of themselves do not exist,—what remains? It is all one; "X" and "Y" are one. It is only this mind, this form, that has limited them apparently, and made them differ as internal and external world. "X" and "Y" are both unknown and unknowable. We cannot attribute any quality to them. As such they are both the same. That which is qualitiless and attributeless and absolute must be one. There cannot be two absolutes. When there are no qualities there can be only One. "X" and "Y" are both without qualities because they take qualities only in the mind, therefore this "X" and "Y" are one.

The whole universe is One. There is only One Self in the universe, only One Existence, and that One Existence, when it is passing through the forms of time, space and causation, is called Intelligence, Self-consciousness, fine matter, gross matter, etc. All physical and mental forms, everything in the universe is that One, appearing in various ways. When a little bit of it gets into this network of time, space and causation, it apparently takes forms ; remove the network and it is all One. This whole universe is all one, and is called in the Advaitist philosophy

Brahman. *Brahman* appearing behind the universe is called God ; appearing behind the little universe—the microcosm, is the soul. This very "Self" or Âtman therefore is God in man. There is only one *Purusha*, and He is called God, and when God and man are analyzed they are one, The universe is you yourself, the undivided you ; you are throughout this universe. "In all hands you work, through all mouths you eat, through all nostrils you breathe, through all minds you think."* The whole universe is you ; this universe is your body ; you are the universe, both formed and unformed. You are the soul of the universe, its body also. You are God, you are the angels, you are man, you are the animals, you are the plants, you are the minerals, you are everything ; all manifestation is you. Whatever exists is you—the *real* "You"—the one undivided Self—

* Compare Gita XIII. 13.

not the little, limited personality that you have been regarding as yourself.

The question now arises,—how have you, the Infinite Being, become broken into parts, as Mr. So-and-So, the animals and so on? The answer is that all this division is only apparent. We know that the infinite cannot be divided, therefore this idea—that you are a part only—has no reality, and never will have ; and this idea that you are Mr. So-and-so was never true at any time ; it is but a dream. Know this and be free. That is the Advaitist conclusion. "I am neither the mind, nor the body, nor am I the organs ; I am Existence-Knowledge-Bliss Absolute ; I am He, I am He."* This is knowledge, and everything besides this is ignorance. Everything that is, is but ignorance, the result of ignorance. Where is knowledge for me, for I am knowledge itself! Where

* SankarAcharya's Nirvan Satak I

is life for me, for I am life itself! Life is a secondary manifestation of my nature. I am sure I live, for I am life, the one Being. Nothing exists except through me, and in me, and as me. I am manifested as the elements, but I am the One, free. Who seeks freedom? Nobody seeks freedom. If you think that you are bound, you remain bound; you make your own bondage. If you realize that you are free, you are free this moment. This is knowledge, the knowledge of freedom and freedom is the goal of all nature.

IV

THE FREE SOUL

We have seen that the analysis of the *Sânkhyas* stops with the duality of existence, *Prakriti* and souls. There are an infinite number of souls, which, being simple, cannot die, and must therefore be separate from *Prakriti*. *Prakriti* in itself changes and manifests all these phenomena, and the soul, according to the *Sânkhyas* is inactive. It is a simple by itself, and *Prakriti* works out all these phenomena for the liberation of the soul, and liberation consists in the soul's discriminating that it is not Nature. At the same time we have seen that the *Sânkhyas* were bound to admit that every soul was omnipresent. Being a simple the soul cannot be limited, because all limitation comes either through time, space, or causation. The soul being entirely beyond these cannot have any limitation. To have limitation one must be in space, which means that it must have a body, and that which has a body must be in *Prakriti*. If the soul had form, it would be identified with *Prakriti*; therefore the soul is formless, and that which is formless cannot be said to exist here, there, or anywhere. It must be omnipresent. Beyond this the *Sânkhya* philosophy does not go.

The first argument of the Vedantists against this is that this analysis is not a perfect one. If this *Prakriti* be a simple, and the soul is also a simple, there will be two simples, and all the arguments that apply in the case of the soul to show that it is omnipresent, will apply equally in the case of *Prakriti*, and that too will be beyond all time, space, and causation, and as the result there will be no change or manifestation. Then will come the difficulty of having two simples, or two absolutes, which is impossible. What is the solution of the Vedantist ? His solution is that, it requires some sentient being as the motive power behind, to make the mind think and *Prakriti* work, because *Prakriti* in all its modifications, from gross matter up to *Mahat* (Intelligence) is simply insentient. Now, says the Vedantist, this sentient being which is behind the whole universe is what we call *God*, and consequently this universe is not different from Him. It is He Himself who has become this universe. He not only is the instrumental cause of this universe, but also the material cause. Cause is never different from effect, the effect is but the cause reproduced in another form. We see that every day. So this Being is the cause of *Prakriti*. All the forms and phases of Vedânta, either dualistic, or qualified-monistic, or monistic, first take this position,

—that God is not only the instrumental but also the efficient cause of this universe, that everything which exists is He. The second step in Vedânta is that these souls are also a part of God, one spark of that Infinite Fire. "As from a mass of fire millions of small particles fly, even so from this Ancient One have come all these souls."* So far so good, but it does not yet satisfy. What is meant by a part of the Infinite? The Infinite is indivisible; there cannot be parts of the Infinite. The Absolute cannot be divided. What is meant therefore by the expression that all these sparks are from Him? The Advaitist, the non-dualistic Vedantist, solves the problem by maintaining that there is really no part, that each soul is really not a part of the Infinite, but actually *is* the Infinite *Brahman*. Then how can there be so many souls? The sun reflected from millions of

* Mundakopanishada II. 1.

globules of water appears to be millions of suns, and in each globule is a miniature picture of the sun-form ; so all these souls are but reflections and not real. They are not the real " I " which is the God of this universe, the one undivided Being of the universe. And so all these little different beings, men, animals, etc., are but reflections, and not real. They are simply illusory reflections upon *Prakriti*. There is but one Infinite Being in the universe, and that Being appears as you and as I, but this appearance of division is after all delusion. He has not been divided, but only appears to be divided. This apparent division is caused by looking at Him through the network of time, space, and causation. When I look at God through the network of time, space, and causation, I see Him as the material world. When I look at Him from a little higher plane, yet through the same network, I see Him as an animal, a little higher as a man, a little higher as a god, but yet He is the One Infinite Being of the universe, and that Being we are. I am That, and you are That. Not parts of It, but the whole of It. "It is the Eternal Knower standing behind the whole phenomena; He, Himself is the phenomena." He is both the subject and the object, He is the "I" and the "You." How is this? "How to know the knower?"* The Knower cannot know himself. I see everything but cannot see myself. The Self, the Knower, the Lord of all, the Real Being, is the cause of all the vision that is in the universe, but it is impossible for Him to see Himself or know Himself, excepting through reflection. You cannot see your own face excepting in a mirror, and so the Self cannot see its own nature until it is reflected, and this whole universe therefore

* Brihadâranyaka Upanishada V. 15.

is the Self trying to realize Itself. This reflection is thrown back first from the protoplasm, then from plants and animals, and so on and on from better and better reflectors, until the best reflector,—the perfect man,—is reached. Just as a man who, wanting to see his face, looks first in a little pool of muddy water, and sees just an outline. Then he comes to clearer water, and sees a better image, then to a piece of shining metal, and sees a still better image, and at last to a looking-glass, and sees himself reflected as he is. Therefore the perfect man is the highest reflection of that Being, who is both subject and object. You now find why man instinctively worships everything, and how perfect men are instinctively worshipped as God in every country. You may talk as you like, but it is they who are bound to be worshipped. That is why men worship Incarnations, such as Christ or Buddha.

They are the most perfect manifestations of the eternal Self. They are much higher than all the conceptions of God that you or I can make. A perfect man is much higher than such conceptions. In him the circle becomes complete; the subject and the object become one. In him all delusions go away and in their place comes the realization that he has always been that perfect Being. How came this bondage then? How was it possible for this perfect Being to degenerate into the imperfect? How was it possible that the free became bound? The *Advaitist* says he was never bound, but was always free. Various clouds of various colors come before the sky. They remain there a minute and then pass away. It is the same eternal blue sky stretching there forever. The sky never changes; it is the cloud that is changing. So you are always perfect, eternally perfect. Nothing ever changes your nature, or ever will. All these ideas that I am imperfect, I am a man, or a woman, or a sinner, or I am the mind, I have thought, I will think, all are hallucinations ; you never think, you never had a body ; you never were imperfect. You are the blessed Lord of this universe, the one Almighty ruler of everything that is and ever will be, the one mighty ruler of these suns and stars and moons and earths and plants, and all the little bits of our universe. It is through you the sun shines, and the stars shed their lustre, and the earth becomes beautiful. It is through your blessedness that they all love and are attracted to each other. You are in all, and you are all. Whom to avoid, and whom to take ? You are the all in all. When this knowledge comes delusion immediately vanishes.

I was once travelling in the desert in India. I travelled for over a month and always found the most beautiful landscapes before me, beautiful blending of trees and lakes and all things. One day I was very thirsty and I wanted to have a drink at one of these lakes, but when I approached that lake it vanished. Immediately with a blow came into my brain the idea that this was a mirage about which I had read all my life, and then I remembered and smiled at my folly, that for the last month all the beautiful landscapes and lakes I had been seeing were this mirage, but I could not distinguish them then. The next morning I again began my march ; there was the lake and the landscape, but with it immediately came the idea, "This is a mirage." Once known it had lost its powers of illusion. So this illusion of the universe will break one day. The whole of this will vanish, melt away. This is realization. Philosophy is no joke or talk. It will be realized ; this body will vanish, this earth and everything will vanish, this idea that

I am the body, or the mind, will for some time vanish, or if the *Karma* is ended it will disappear never to come back ; but if one part of the *Karma* remains,—as a potter's wheel after the potter has finished the pot, will sometimes go on from the past momentum—the body, when this delusion has vanished altogether, will go on for some time. Again this world will come, men and women and animals will come, just as the mirage came the next day, but not with the same force, for along with it will come the idea that I know its nature now, and it will cause no bondage, no more pain, nor grief, nor misery. Whenever anything miserable will come, the mind will be able to say, "I know you as hallucination." When a man has reached that state he is called *jivan mukta*, "living free," free even while living. The aim and end in this life for the *Jnâna Yogi* is to become this *jivan mukta*, living freedom.

He is *jivan mukta* who can live in this world without being attached. He is like the lotus leaves in water, which are never wet by the water. He is the highest of human beings, nay, the highest of all beings, for he has realized his identity with the Absolute, he has realized that he is one with God. So long as you think you have the least difference from God, fear will seize you, but when you have known that you are He, that there is no difference, entirely no difference, between you and Him, that you are all of Him, and the whole of Him, all fear ceases. "There who sees whom ? Who worships whom ? Who talks to whom ? Who hears whom ? Where one sees another, where one talks to another, where one hears another, it is in law. Where none sees none, where none speaks to none that is the highest, that is the great, that is the *Brahman*."* Being

* Brihadâranyaka Upanishada V. 15.

That, you are always That. What will become of the world then ? What good shall we do to the world ? Such questions do not arise. "What becomes of my gingerbread if I become old ?" says the baby. "What becomes of my marbles if I grow, so I will not grow," says the boy. "What will become of my dolls if I grow old ?" says the little child. It is the same question in connection with this world ; it has no existence in the past, present, or future. If we have known the *Âtman* as It is, if we have known that there is nothing else but this *Âtman*, that everything else is but a dream, with no existence in reality, then this world with its poverties, its miseries, its wickedness and its goodness will cease to disturb us. If they do not exist, for whom and for what shall we take trouble ? This is what the *Jnâna Yogis* teach. Therefore, dare to be free, dare to go as far as your thought leads, and dare to carry that out in your life. It is very hard to come to *jnânam.* It is for the bravest and most daring, who dare to smash all idols, not only intellectual, but also of the senses.

This body is not I ; it must go. All sorts of curious things may come out of this teaching. A man stands up and says "I am not the body, therefore my headache must be cured !"—but where is the headache if not in his body ? Let a thousand headaches and a thousand bodies come and go. What is that to me ? "I have neither birth nor death ; father nor mother I never had ; friends and foes I have none, because they are all I ; I am my own friend and I am my own enemy ; I am Existence-Knowledge-Bliss Absolute ; I am He, I am He."* If in a thousand bodies I am suffering from fever and other ills, in millions of bodies I am healthy. If in a

* Sankarâchârya's Nirvân Satak.

thousand bodies I am starving, in other thousand bodies I am feasting. If in thousands of bodies I am suffering misery, in thousands of bodies I am happy. Who shall blame whom, who praise whom? "Whom to seek, whom to avoid?" I seek none, nor avoid any, for I am all the universe, I praise myself, I blame myself, I suffer for myself, I am happy at my own will, I am free. This is the *Jnâni*, brave and daring. Let the whole universe tumble down; he smiles and says it never existed, it was all hallucination. Thus he sees the universe really disappear before his eyes and questions wondering "Where was it? Whether has it melted away?"

Before going into the practical part, we will take up one more intellectual question. So far the logic is tremendously rigorous. If a man reasons, there is no place for him to stand until he comes to this, that there is but One Existence, that everything else is nothing. There is no other way left for rational mankind but to take this view. But how is it that what is infinite, ever perfect, ever blessed, Existence-Knowledge-Bliss Absolute has come under these delusions? It is the same question that has been asked all the world over in all times. In the vulgar form the question becomes "How did sin come into this world?" This is the most vulgar and sensuous form of the question, and the other is the more philosophic form, but the answer is the same. The same question has been asked in various grades and fashions, but in its lower forms it finds no solution, because the stories of apples and serpents and women do not give the explanation. In that state, the question is childish and so is the answer. But the question has assumed very high proportions now. "How this illusion came?" and the answer is as fine. The answer is that we cannot expect any answer to an impossible question. The very question is impossible in terms. You have no right to ask that question. Why? What is perfection? That which is beyond time, space and causation. That is perfect. Then you ask how the perfect became imperfect. In logical language the question may be put in this form—"How did that which is beyond causation become caused?" You contradict yourself. You first admit it is beyond causation, and then ask what causes it. Questions can only be asked within the limits of causation. As far as time and space and causation extend, so far can this question be asked. But beyond that it will be nonsense to ask it, because the question is illogical. Within time, space and causation it can never be answered, and what answer may lie beyond these limits can only be known when we have transcended them, therefore the wise will let this question rest. When a man is ill, he devotes himself to curing his disease, without insisting that he must first learn how he came to have it.

There is another form of this question, a little lower, but more practical and illustrative. What produced this delusion? Can any reality produce delusion? Certainly not. We see that one delusion produces another, and so on. It is delusion always that produces delusion. It is disease that produces disease, and not health that produces disease. The wave is the same thing as the water, the effect is the cause in another form. The effect is delusion, and therefore the cause must be delusion. What produced this delusion? Another delusion. And so on without beginning. The only question that remains for you to ask is, does not this admission break your monism, because you get two existences in the universe, one yourself, and the other the delusion? The answer is,—

delusion cannot be called an existence. Thousands of dreams come into your life, but do not form any part of your life. Dreams come and go ; they have no existence ; to call delusion existence will be sophistry. Therefore there is only one individual existence in the universe, ever free, and ever blessed, and that is what you are. This is the last conclusion reached by the *Advaitists.* It may then be asked, what becomes of all these various forms of worship ? They will remain ; they are simply groping in the dark for light, and through this groping light will come. We have just seen that the Self cannot see Itself. All our knowledge is within the network of *Mâyâ* (unreality), and beyond that is freedom. Within the network there is slavery, it is all under law. Beyond that there is no law. So far as the universe is concerned, existence is ruled by law, and beyond that is freedom. As long as you are in the network of time, space and causation, to say you are free is nonsense, because in that network all is under rigorous law, sequence and consequence. Every thought that you think is caused, every feeling has been caused; to say that the will is free is sheer nonsense. It is only when the infinite existence comes, as it were, into this network of *Mâyâ* that it takes the form of will. Will is a portion of that being caught in the network of *Mâyâ*, and therefore "free-will" is a misnomer. It means nothing,—sheer nonsense. So is all this talk about freedom. There is no freedom in *Mâyâ*.

Every one is as much bound in thought, word, deed, and mind, as a piece of stone or this table. That I talk to you now is as rigorously in causation as that you listen to me. There is no freedom until you go beyond *Mâyâ*. That is the real freedom of the soul. Men, however sharp and intellectual, however clearly they see the force of the logic that nothing here can be free, are all compelled to think they are free; they cannot help. No work can go on until we begin to say we are free. It means that the freedom we talk about is the glimpse of the blue sky through the clouds, and that the real freedom,—the blue sky itself,—is behind. True freedom cannot exist in the midst of this delusion, this hallucination, this nonsense of the world, this universe of the senses, body and mind. All these dreams, without beginning or end, uncontrolled and uncontrollable, ill-adjusted, broken, inharmonious, form our idea of this universe. In a dream, when you see a giant with twenty heads chasing you, and you are flying from him, you do not think it is inharmonious; you think it is proper and right. So is this law. All that you call law is simply chance without meaning. In this dream state you call it law. Within *Mâyâ*, so far as this law of time, space and causation exists, there is no freedom, and all these various forms of worship are within this *Mâyâ*. The idea of God and the ideas of brute and of man are within this *Mâyâ*, and as such equally hallucinations; all of them are dreams. But you must take care not to argue like some extraordinary men of whom we hear at the present time. They say the idea of God is a delusion, but the idea of this world is true. Both ideas stand or fall by the same logic. He alone has the right to be an atheist who denies this world, as well as the other. The same argument is for both. The same mass of delusion extends from God to the lowest animal, from a blade of grass to the Creator. They stand or fall by the same logic. The same person who sees falsity in the idea of God ought also to see it in the idea of his own body, or his own mind. When God vanishes, then also vanish the body and mind, and when both vanish, that which is the Real Existence remains forever. "There the eyes cannot go, nor the speech, nor the mind. We cannot see it, neither know it." And we now understand that so far as speech and thought and knowledge, and intellect go, it is all within this *Mâyâ*, within bondage. Beyond that is Reality. There neither thought, nor mind, nor speech, can reach.

So far it is intellectually all right, but then comes the practice. The real work in these classes is the practice. Are any practices necessary to realize this one-ness? Most decidedly. It is not that you become this *Brahman*. You are already that. It is not that you are going to become God or perfect; you are already perfect, and whenever you think you are not, it is a delusion. This delusion which says that you are Mr. So-and-So, or Mrs. So-and-So, can be got rid of by another delusion, and that is practice. Fire will eat fire, and you can use one delusion to conquer another delusion. One cloud will come and brush away another cloud, and then both will go away. What are these practices then? We must always bear in mind that we are not going to be free, but are free already. Every idea that we are bound is a delusion. Every idea that we are happy or unhappy, is a tremendous delusion; and another delusion will come,—that we shall have to work and worship and struggle to be free,—and this will chase out the first delusion, and then both will stop.

The fox is considered very unholy by the Mohammedans, and so is the dog by the Hindus. So, if a fox or a dog touches any bit of food it has to be thrown out, it cannot be eaten by any man. In a certain Mohammedan house a fox entered and took a little bit of food from the table, ate it up and fled. The man was a poor man, and had prepared a very nice feast for himself, and that feast was made unholy, and he could not eat it. So he went to a *Mulla*, a priest, and said: "This has happened to me; a fox came and took a mouthful out of my meal; what can be done? I had prepared a feast and wanted so much to eat it, and now comes this fox and destroys the whole thing." The *Mulla* thought for a minute, and then found only one solution and said: "The only way is for you to get a dog, and make him eat a bit out of the same plate. Now because dogs and foxes are eternally quarrelling, the food that was left by the fox will go into your stomach, and that not eaten by the dog will go there, and destroy each other and thus all will be purified." We are very much in the same predicament. This is an hallucination that we are imperfect, and we take up another, that we have to practice to become perfect. Then one will chase the other, as we can use one thorn to extract another and then throw both away. There are people for whom it is sufficient knowledge to hear, "Thou art That." With a flash this universe goes away and the real nature shines, but others have to struggle hard to get rid of this idea of bondage.

The first question is, who are fit to become *Jnâna Yogis?* Those who are equipped with these requisites. First, renunciation of all fruits of work and of all enjoyments in this life or another life. If you are the creator of this universe whatever you desire you will have, because you will create it for yourself. It is only a question of time. Some get it immediately; with others the past *samskâras* (impressions) stand in the way of getting their desires. We give the first place to desires for enjoyment, either in this or another life. Deny there is any life at all, because life is only another name for death. Deny that you are a living being. Who cares for life ? Life is one of these hallucinations and death is its counterpart. Joy is one part of these hallucinations, and misery the other part, and so on. What have you to do with life or death ? These are all creations of the mind. This is called giving up desires of enjoyment either in this life or another.

Then comes controlling the mind, calming it so that it will not break into waves and have all sorts of desires ; holding the mind steady, not allowing it to get into waves from external or internal causes, controlling the mind perfectly just by the power of will. The *Jnâna Yogi* does not take any one of these physical helps, or mental helps, simply philosophic reasoning, knowledge and his own will, these are the instrumentality he believes in. Next comes *Titikshâ*, forbearance, bearing all miseries without murmuring, without complaining. When an injury comes, do not mind it. If a tiger comes, stand there. Who flies? There are men who practice *titikshâ*, and succeed in it. There are men who sleep on the banks of the Ganges in the mid-summer sun of India, and in winter float in the waters of the Ganges for a whole day; they do not care. Men sit in the snow of the Himâlayas, and do not care to wear any garment. What is heat? What is cold? Let things come and go, what is that to me, I am not the body. It is hard to believe this in these Western countries, but it is better to know that it is done. Just as your people are brave to jump at the mouth of a cannon, or into the midst of the battle-field, so our people are brave to think and act out their philosophy. They give up their lives for it. "I am Existence-Knowledge-

Bliss Absolute; I am He; I am He." Just as the Western ideal is to keep up luxury in practical life, so ours is to keep up the highest form of spirituality, to demonstrate that religion is not merely frothy words, but can be carried out, every bit of it, in this life. This is *titikshâ*, to bear everything, not to complain of anything. I myself have seen men who say "I am the soul; what is the universe to me? Neither pleasure, nor pain, nor virtue, nor vice, nor heat, nor cold are anything to me." That is *titikshâ*; not running after the enjoyments of the body. What is religion? To pray: "give me this and that"? Foolish ideas of religion it is! Those who believe them have no true idea of God and soul. My Master used to say the vulture rises high and high until he becomes a speck, but his eye is always in the piece of rotten carrion on the earth. After all, what is the result of your ideas of religion? To cleanse the streets, and have more bread and clothes. Who cares for bread and clothes? Millions come and go every minute. Who cares? Why care for the joys and vicissitudes of this little world? Go beyond that if you dare; go beyond law, let the whole universe vanish, and stand alone. "I am Existence-Absolute, Knowledge-Absolute, Bliss-Absolute; I am He; I am He."

V

ONE EXISTENCE APPEARING AS MANY

We have seen how *Vairâgyam*, or renunciation, is the turning point in all these various *Yogas*. The *Karmi* (worker) renounces the fruits of his work. The *Bhakta* (devotee) renounces all little loves for the almighty and omnipresent love. The *Yogi* renounces his experiences, because his philosophy is that the whole Nature, although it is for the experience of the soul, at last brings him to know that he is not in Nature, but eternally separate from Nature. The *Jnâni* (philosopher) renounces everything, because his philosophy is that Nature never existed, neither in the past, present nor future. We have also seen how the question of utility cannot be asked in these higher themes; it is very absurd to raise the question of utility, and even if it be raised after a proper analysis what do we find in this question? The ideal of happiness, that which brings man greater happiness is of greater utility to him than those things which do not improve his material conditions or bring him such great happiness. All the sciences are for this one end, to bring happiness to humanity and that which brings the larger amount of happiness, mankind takes and gives up that which brings a lesser amount of happiness. We have seen how happiness is either in the body, or in the mind, or in the *Âtman*. With animals, and in the lowest of human beings, who are very much like animals, happiness is all in the body. No man can eat with the same pleasure as a famished dog, or a wolf; so, in the dog and the wolf the ideal of happiness is concerned entirely with the body. In men we find a higher plane of happiness, that of thought, and in the *Jnâni* there is the highest plane of happiness in the Self, the *Âtman*. So to the philosopher this knowledge of the Self is of the highest utility, because it gives him the highest happiness possible. Sense gratifications or physical things cannot be of the highest utility to him because he does not find in them the same pleasure that he finds in knowledge itself; and after all, knowledge is the one goal, and is really the highest happiness that we know. All who work in ignorance are, as it were, "the draught animals of the *devas*." The word *deva* is here used in the sense of a wise man. All the people that work, and toil, and labor like machines do not really enjoy life, but it is the wise man who enjoys. A rich man buys a picture at a cost of a hundred thousand dollars perhaps, but it is the man who understands art that enjoys it; and if the buyer is without knowledge of art it is useless to him, he is only the owner. All over the world, it is the wise man who enjoys the happiness of the world. The ignorant man never enjoys; he has to work for others unconsciously.

Thus far we have seen the theories of these Advaitist philosophers, how there is but one *Âtman;* there cannot be two. We have seen how in the whole of this universe there is but One Existence, and that One Existence when seen through the senses is called the world, the world of matter. When It is seen through the mind It is called the world of thoughts and ideas, and when It is seen as it is, then It appears as the One Infinite Being. You must bear this in mind; it is not that there is a soul in man, although I had to take that for granted in order to explain it at first, but that there is only One Existence, and that one the *Âtman*, the Self, and when this is perceived through the senses, through sense imageries, It is called the body. When It is perceived through thought, It is called the mind. When It is perceived in Its own nature, It appears as the *Âtman*, the One Only Existence. So, it is not that there are three things in one, the body and the mind and the Self,—although that was a convenient way of putting it in the course of explanation—but all is that *Âtman*, and that one Being is sometimes called the body, sometimes the mind, and sometimes the Self, according to different visions. There is but one Being which the ignorant call the world. When a man goes higher in knowledge he calls the very same Being the world of thought. Again when perfect knowledge comes, all illusions vanish, and man finds it is all nothing but *Âtman*. "I am that One Existence"—this is the last conclusion. There are neither three nor two in the universe ; it is all One. That One, under the illusion of *Mâyâ* is seen as many, just as a rope is seen as a snake. It is the very rope that is seen as a snake There are not two things there, a rope separate and a snake separate. No man sees two things there. Dualism and non-dualism are very good philosophic terms, but in perfect perception we never perceive the real and the false at the same time. We are all born monists, we cannot help it. We always perceive the one. When we perceive the rope, we do not perceive the snake at all, and when we see the snake, we do not see the rope at all ; it has vanished. When you see illusion, you do not see real men. Suppose one of your friends is coming from a distance in the street ; you know him very well, but through the haze and mist that is before you, you think it is another man. When you see your friend as another man, you do not see your friend at all, he has vanished. You are perceiving only one person: For suppose your friend is A.; when you perceive A. as B. you do not see A. at all. So in each case you perceive only one. When you see yourself as a body, you are body and nothing else, and that is the perception of the vast majority of mankind. They may talk of soul and mind, and all such things, but what they perceive is the physical form, the touch, taste, vision, and so on. Again, with certain men, in certain states of consciousness, they perceive themselves as thought. You know, of course, the story told of Sir Humphrey Davy, who was making experiments before his class with laughing-gas, and suddenly one of the tubes broke, and the gas escaping, he breathed it in. For some moments he remained like a statue. Afterwards he told his class that when he was in that state, he actually perceived that the whole world is made up of ideas. The gas, for a time, made him forget the consciousness of the body, and that very thing which he was seeing as the body, he began to perceive as ideas. When the consciousness rises still higher, when this little puny consciousness is transcended for ever, that which is the Reality behind shines, and we see it as the One Existence-Knowledge-Bliss, the one *Âtman*, the Universal Being. "One that is only knowledge itself, One that is bliss itself, beyond all compare, beyond all limit, ever free, never bound, infinite as the sky, undivided and unchangeable,—such an One will manifest Himself in your heart in meditation."*

How does the Advaitist theory explain all these various phases of heavens and hells and all these various ideas we find in all religions? When a man dies it is said

* Vivekachudamani 410.

that he goes to heaven or hell, goes here or there, or that when a man dies he is born again in another body, either in heaven or in another world, or somewhere. These are all hallucinations. Nobody is ever born or dies, really speaking. There is neither heaven nor hell, nor this world ; all three never really existed. Tell a child a lot of ghost stories, and let him go out into the street in the evening. There is a little stump of a tree. What does the child see ? A ghost, with hands stretched out, ready to seize him. Suppose a man comes from the corner of the street, wanting to meet his sweetheart ; he sees that stump of the tree as the girl. A policeman coming from the street corner sees the stump as a thief. The thief sees it as a policeman. It is the same stump of a tree that was seen in various ways. The stump is the reality, and the visions of the stump are the projections of the various minds. There is one Being, this Self; It neither comes nor goes. When a man is ignorant, he wants to go to heaven or some place, and all his life he has been thinking and thinking of this, and when this earth dream vanishes he sees this world as a heaven, with *devas* and angels flying about, and all such things. If a man all his life desires to meet his forefathers he gets them all, from Adam downwards, because he creates them. If a man is still more ignorant and has always been frightened by fanatics with ideas of hell, when he dies he will see this very world as hell, with all sorts of punishments. All that is meant by dying or being born is simply a change in the plane of vision. Neither do you move, nor does that move upon which you project your vision. You are the permanent, the unchangeable. How can you go and come? It is imposible; you are omnipresent. The sky never moves, but the clouds move over the surface of the sky, and we think that the sky itself moves. Just as you go into a railway train, and you think the land is moving. It is not so, but it is the train which is moving. So you are where you are while this dream, like these various clouds, moves. One dream follows another without connection. There is no such thing as law or connection in this world, but we are thinking that there is a great deal of connection. All of you have probably read "Alice in Wonderland." It is the most wonderful book for children written in this century. When I read it I was delighted, it was always in my head to write that sort of a book for children. What pleased me most in it was that what you think most incongruous, that is there—the want of all connection. One idea comes and jumps into another, without any connection. When you were children you thought that to be the most wonderful connecticn. So this man brought back his thoughts of childhood, perfectly connected to him as a child, and composed this book for children: while many of these books which men write, trying to make children swallow their own ideas as men are nonsense. We too are grown up children, that is all. The world is the same unconnected thing,—"Alice in Wonderland,"—with no connection whatever. When we see things happen a number of times in a certain sequence, we call it cause and effect, and say that the thing will happen again. When this dream will change another dream will seem quite as connected as this. When we dream, the things we see all seem to be connected; during the dream we never think they are incongruous; it is only when we wake that we see the want of connection. So when we wake from this dream of the world and compare it with the Reality, it will all be found incongruous nonsense, a mass of incongruity passing before us, we do not know whence or whither; but we know it will end. And this is called *Mâyâ*. Like masses of fleeting, fleecy clouds is all this changing existence, and the sun itself, the unchanging, is you. When you look at that unchanging Existence from the outside, you call it God, and when you look at it from the inside you call it yourself. It is but one. There is no God separate from you, no God higher than you, the real "you." All the Gods are little beings to you, all the ideas of God and Father in heaven are but your reflection. God Himself is your image. "God created man after His own image"—that is wrong. Man creates God after his own image—this is right. Throughout the universe we are creating gods after our own image. We create the god, and fall down at his feet and worship ; and when this dream comes, we love it !

This is a good point to understand,—that the sum and substance of this morning's lecture is that there is but One Existence, and that One Existence seen through different mediums appears either as earth, or heaven, or hell, or God, or ghosts, or men or demons, or world, or all these things. But—"he who sees that One, who never changes among these diverse changing things, he who sees that One Life in this floating universe of death, he who realizes within himself the One who fulfils the desires of these many, unto him belongs eternal peace ; unto none else, unto none else."* This One Existence has to be realized. How, is the next question. How is it to be realized ? How is this dream to be broken, how shall we wake up from this dream that we are little men and women, and all

* Katha Upanishada V. 13.

such things ? We are the Infinite Being of the universe, and have become materialized into these little beings, men and women, depending upon the sweet word of one man, or the angry word of another man and so forth. What a terrible dependence, what a terrible slavery ! I who am beyond all pleasure and pain, whose reflection is the whole universe, little bits of whose life are the suns and moons and stars,—I am held down as a terrible slave. If you pinch my body I feel pain. If one says a kind word I begin to rejoice. Look at my condition,—slave of the body, slave of the mind, slave of the world, slave of a good word, slave of a bad word, slave of passion, slave of happiness, slave of life, slave of death, slave of every thing. This slavery has to be broken. How ? "This *Âtman* has first to be heard, then reasoned upon and then meditated upon."* This is the method

* Brihadâranyaka Upanishada V. 6.

of the Advaita *Jnâni*. The truth has to be heard, then reflected upon and then to be constantly asserted. Think always—"I am *Brahman*" ; every other thought must be cast aside as weakening. Cast aside every thought that says that you are men or women. Let body go, and mind go, and gods go, and ghosts go. Let everything go but that One Existence. "Where one hears another, where one sees another, that is but small ; where one does not here another, where one does not see another, that is infinite."* That is the highest, where the subject and the object become one. When I am the listener and I am the speaker, when I am the teacher and I am the taught, when I am the creator and I am the created,—then alone fear ceases ; for there is not another to make us afraid. There is nothing but myself, what can frighten

* Chhândogya Upanishada XXIV.

me? This is to be heard day after day. Get rid of all other thoughts. Everything else must be thrown aside, and this is to be repeated continually, poured through the ears until it reaches the heart, until every nerve and muscle, every drop of blood tingles with the idea that I am He, I am He. Even at the gate of death say "I am He." There was a man in India, a *Sannyâsin*, who used to repeat "*Shivoham*" ("I am Bliss Eternal"), and a tiger jumped on him one day and dragged him away and killed him, and as long as he was living the sound came "*Shivoham, Shivoham.*" Even at the gate of death, in the greatest danger, in the thick of the battle-field, at the bottom of the ocean, on the tops of the highest mountains, in the thickest of the forest, tell yourself "I am He, I am He." Day and night say "I am He." It is the greatest strength; it is religion. "The weak will never reach the *Âtman*."* Never say: "O Lord, I am a miserable sinner." Who shall help you? Yor are the help of the universe. What in this universe can help you? Where is the man, or the god, or the demon to help you? What can prevail over you? You are the god of the universe; where can you seek for help? Never help came from anywhere but from yourself. In your ignorance, every prayer that you made and that was answered, you thought was answered by some Being, but you answered the prayer yourself, unknowingly. The help came from yourself, and you fondly imagined that some one was sending help to you. There is no help for you outside of yourself; you are the creator of the universe. Like the silkworm you have built a cocoon around yourself. Who will save you? Cut your own cocoon and come out as the beautiful

* Mundaka Upânishada. III. 2—4.

butterfly, as the free soul. Then alone you will see Truth. Ever tell yourself "I am He." These are words that will burn up the dross that is in the mind, words that will bring out the tremendous energy which is within you already, the infinite power which is sleeping in your heart. This is to be brought out by constantly hearing the truth and nothing else. Wherever there is thought of weakness, approach not the place. Avoid all weakness if you want to be *Jnâni*.

Before you begin to practise, clear your mind of all doubts. Fight and reason and argue, and when you have established it in your mind that this and this alone can be the truth and nothing else, do not argue any more ; close your mouth. Hear not argumentation, neither argue yourself. What is the use of any more arguments ? You have satisfied yourself, you have decided the question. What remains ?

The truth has now to be realized, therefore why waste valuable time in vain arguments ? The truth has now to be meditated upon and every idea that strengthens you must be taken up and every thought that weakens you must be rejected. The *Bhakta* meditates upon forms and images and all such things and upon God. This is the natural process, but a slower one. The *Yogi* meditates upon various centres in his body and manipulates powers in his mind. The *Jnâni* says the mind does not exist, neither the body. This idea of the body and of the mind must go, must be driven off ; therefore it is foolish to think of them. It would be like trying to cure one ailment by bringing in another. His meditation therefore is the most difficult one, the negative ; he denies everything, and what is left is the Self. This is the most analytical way. The *Jnâni* wants to tear away the universe from the Self by the sheer force of analysis. It is very easy to say, "I am a *Jnâni*," but very hard to be one really. "The way is long ; it is, as it were, walking on the sharp edge of a razor, yet despair not. Awake, arise, and stop not until the goal is reached," say the Vedas.*

So what is the meditation of the *Jnâni* ? He wants to rise above every idea of body or mind, to drive away the idea that he is the body. For instance, when I say "I, Swâmi," immediately the idea of the body comes. What must I do then ? I must give the mind a hard blow and say, "No, I am not the body, I am the Self." Who cares if disease comes or death in the most horrible form ? I am not the body. Why make the body nice ? To enjoy the illusion once more ? To continue the slavery ? Let it go, I am not the body. That is the way of the *Jnâni*.

* Katha Upanishada. I. 3—14.

The *Bhakta* says : "The Lord has given me this body that I may safely cross the ocean of life and I must cherish it until the journey is accomplished.' The *Yogi* says : "I must be careful of the body so that I may go on steadily and finally attain liberation." The *Jnâni* feels that he cannot wait, he must reach the goal this very moment. He says : "I am free through eternity, I am never bound ; I am the God of the universe through all eternity. Who shall make me perfect ? I am perfect already." When a man is perfect he sees perfection in others. When he sees imperfection, it is his own mind projecting itself. How can he see imper fection if he has not got it in himself ? So the *Jnâni* does not care for perfection or imperfection. None exists for him. As soon as he is free, he does not see good and evil. Who sees evil and good ? He who has it in himself. Who sees the body ?

He who thinks he is the body. The moment yet get rid of the idea that you are the body, you do not see the world at all. It vanishes forever. The *Jnâni* seeks to tear himself away from this bondage of matter by the force of intellectual conviction. This is the negative way,—the "*neti, neti*" ("not this, not this").

IV

UNITY OF THE SELF

To illustrate the conclusion arrived at in our last lesson, I will read to you from one of the Upanishads* showing how these ideas were taught in India from the most ancient times.

Yajnavalkya was a great sage. You know the rule in India was that every man must give up the world when he became old. So *Yajnavalkya* said to his wife : "My beloved, here is all my money and my possessions, I am going away." She replied : "Sir, if I had this whole earth full of wealth would that give me immortality ?" *Yajnavalkya* said : "No, that cannot be. Your life will be that of the rich, and that will be all, for wealth cannot give you immortality." She replied :

* Brihadâranyaka Upanishada V.

"That through which I shall become immortal, what shall I do to gain that? If you know that, tell. me." *Yajnavalkya* replied: "You have always been my beloved; you are more so now by this question. Come, take your seat, and I will tell you, and when you have heard, meditate upon it." He continued: "It is not for the sake of the husband that the wife loves the husband, but for the sake of the *Âtman* (the Self) that she loves the husband, because she loves the Self. None loves the wife for the sake of the wife, but it is because he loves the Self that he loves the wife. None loves the children for the sake of the children, but because he loves the Self, therefore he loves the children. None loves wealth on account of the wealth, but because he loves the Self, therefore he loves wealth. None loves the Brahmin for the sake of the Brahmin, but because he loves the Self, he loves the Brahmin. So none loves the *Kshatriya* for the sake of the *Kshatriya*, but because he loves the Self. Neither does anyone love the world on account of the world, but because he loves the Self. None similarly loves the gods on account of the gods, but because he loves the Self. None loves anything for that thing's sake, but it is for the Self of that thing that he loves it. This Self therefore, is to be heard, is to be reasoned, and is to be meditated upon. Oh my *Maitreyi*, when that Self has been heard, when that Self has been seen, when that Self has been realized, then all these things become known."

What does this mean ? Before us we find a curious philosophy. That the Self shines through all these various things which we call the world. The statement has been made that every love is selfishness in the lowest sense of the word ; because I love myself, therefore I love another—this cannot be. There have been philosophers too in modern times who have said that self is the only motive power in the world. That is true, and yet it is wrong. This self is but the shadow of that real Self which is behind and love of this little self appears wrong and evil because it is limited. That very love we have for the Self, which is the universe, appears to be evil, as selfishness because it is seen through limitation. Even when a wife loves a husband, whether she knows it or not, she loves the husband for that Self. It is selfishness as it is manifested in the world, but that selfishness is really but a small part of that "Self-ness." Whenever one loves, one has to love in and through the Self.

This Self has to be known. Those that love the Self without knowing what It is, their love is selfishness. Those that love knowing what that Self is, their love is free, they are sages. None loves the Brahmin for the Brahmin, but because he loves the Self, which is appearing through the Brahmin. "Him the Brahmin gives up who sees the Brahmin as separate from the Self. Him the *Kshatriya* gives up who sees the *Kshatriya* as separate from the Self. The world gives him up who sees this world as separate from the Self. The gods give him up who believes the gods to be separate from the Self. All things give him up who knows them as separate from the Self. These Brahmins, these *Kshatriyas*, this world, these gods, whatever exists, everything is that Self." Thus *Yajnavalkya* explains what he means by love. The difficulty comes when we particularize this love. Suppose I love a woman ; as soon as that woman is particularized, is separated, from that *Âtman* (the Self), my love will not be eternal ; it has become selfish and is likely to end in grief, but as soon as I see that woman as the *Âtman*, that love becomes perfect, and will never suffer. So, as soon as you are attached to anything in the universe, detaching it from the universe as a whole —from the *Âtman*—then comes a reaction. With everything that we love outside the Self, grief and misery will be the result. If we enjoy everything in the Self, and as the Self, no misery or reaction will come. This is perfect bliss.

How to come to this ideal? *Yajnavalkya* goes on to tell us the process by which to reach that state. The universe is infinite ; how can we take every particular thing and look at it as the *Âtman*, without knowing the *Âtman* ? "With the drum, at a distance, we cannot conquer the sound produced by it by trying to control the sound waves, but as soon as we come to the drum, and put our hand on it, the sound is conquered. When a conch shell is being blown, we cannot conquer the sound, until we come near and get hold of the shell, and then it is conquered. When the vina is being played, as soon as we come to the vina, we can control the centre of the sound, whence the sound is proceeding. As when some one is burning damp fuel, all sorts of smoke and sparks of various kinds rise, even so from this great One has been breathed out history and knowledge; everything has come out of Him. He breathed out, as it were, all knowledge. As to all water the one goal is the ocean, as to all touch the hand is the one centre, as to all smell the nose is the one centre, as of all taste the tongue is the one centre, as of all form the eyes are the one centre, as of all sounds the ears are the one centre, as of all thought the mind is the one centre, as of all knowledge the heart is the one centre, as of all work the hands are the one centre, as of all speech the organ of speech is the one centre, as the concentrated salt is through and through the waters of the sea, yet not to be seen by the eyes ; even so, oh *Maitreyi*, is this *Âtman* not to be seen by the eyes, yet He permeates this universe. He is everything. He is concentrated knowledge The whole universe rises from Him, and again goes down unto Him. Reaching Him, we go beyond knowledge." We here get the idea that we have all come out just like sparks from Him, and that when we know Him then we go back, and become one with Him again.

Maitreyi became frightened, just as everywhere people become frightened. She said : "Sir, here is exactly where you have thrown a confusion over me. You have frightened me by saying there will be no more gods ; all individuality will be lost. When I reach that stage shall I know that *Âtman* ? Shall I reach the unconscious state and lose my individuality, or will the knowledge remain with me that I know Him? Will there be no one to recognize, no one to feel, no one to love, no one to hate? What will become of me?" "O *Maitreyi!*" replied her husband, "think not that I am speaking of an unconscious state, neither be frightened. This *Âtman* is indestructible, eternal in His essence; the stage where there are two is a lower one. Where there are two there one smells another, one sees another, one hears another, one welcomes another, one thinks of another, one knows another. But when the whole has become that *Âtman*, who is to be smelled by whom, who is to be seen by whom, who is to be heard by whom, who is to be welcomed by whom, who is to be known by whom? Who can know Him by whom everything is known? This *Âtman* can only be described as "*neti, neti*" (not this, not this). Incomprehensible, He cannot be comprehended by the intellect. Unchangeable, He never fades. Unattached, He never gets mixed up with Nature. Perfect, He is beyond all pleasure and pain. Who can know the Knower? By what means can we know Him? By no means; this is the conclusion of the sages, O *Maitreyi!* Going beyond all knowledge, is to attain Him and to attain immortality."

So far the idea is, that it is all One Infinite Being, and in It is the Real Individuality, where there is no more division, no more parts and parcels, no more such low and illusory ideas. And yet, in and through every part of this little individuality is shining that Infinite, the Real Individuality. Everything is a manifestation of the *Âtman.* How to reach to that? *Yajnavalkya* told us in the beginning that—"This *Âtman* is first to be heard, then to be reasoned, then to be meditated upon." Thus far he has spoken about the Self, the *Âtman*, as being the essence of everything in this universe. Then reasoning on the Infinite nature of that Self and the finite nature of the human mind he comes to the conclusion that it is impossible for the finite mind to know the Knower of all—the Self. What is to be done then if we cannot know the Self ? *Yajnavalkya* tells *Maitreyi* that It can be realized, although It cannot be known, and he enters upon a discourse as to how It is to be meditated upon. This universe is helpful to every being and every being is also helping this universe, for they are both part and parcel of each other, the development of the one helps the development of the other ; but to the *Âtman*, the self-effulgent One, nothing can be helpful because It is perfect and infinite. All that is bliss, even in the lowest sense, is but the reflection of It. All that is good is the reflection of that *Âtman*, and when that reflection is less clear it is called evil. When the *Âtman* is less manifested it is called darkness—evil, and when it is more manifested it is called light—goodness. That is all. This good and evil are only a question of degree, the *Âtman* more manifested or less manifested. Just take the example of our own lives. How many things we see in our childhood which we think to be good, but which really are evil, and how many things seem to be evil which are good? How our ideas change! How an idea becomes higher and higher! What we thought very good at one time, we do not think that so good now. Thus good and evil depend on the development of our minds, and do not exist objectively. The difference is only in the degree. All is a manifestation of that *Âtman*; It is being manifested in everything, only when the manifestation is very poor we call it evil, and when it is clearer we call it good. That *Ātman* Itself is beyond both good and evil. So everything that is in the universe in first to be meditated upon as all good, because it is a manifestation of that perfect One. He is neither evil nor good ; He is perfect and the perfect can be only one. The good can be many, and the evil many, there will be degrees of variation between the good and the evil ; but the perfect is only one, and that perfect One when seen through certain kinds of covering we call different degrees of good, and when seen through other kinds we call evil. Our ideas of good and evil as to distinct things are mere superstition. There is only more good and less good and the less good we call evil. These mistaken ideas of good and evil have produced all sorts of dualistic delusions. They have gone deep into the hearts of human beings, terrorizing men and women in all ages. All the hatred with which we hate others is caused by these foolish ideas which we have imbibed since our childhood. Our judgment of humanity has become entirely false ; we have made this beautiful earth a hell, but as soon as we can give up these false ideas of good and evil, it will become a heaven.

"This earth is blissful ('sweet' is the literal translation) to all beings, and all beings are sweet to this earth ; they all help each other. And all this sweetness is from the *Âtman*, that effulgent, immortal One." That one sweetness is manifesting itself in various ways. Wherever there is any love, any sweetness in any human being, either in a saint or a sinner, either in an angel or a murderer, either in the body or the mind or the senses, it is all He. How can there be anything but that One ? Whatever is the lowest physical enjoyment is He, and the highest spiritual enjoyment is also He. There is no sweetness but He. Thus says *Yajnavalkya.* When you come to that state, and look upon all things with the same eyes; when you see in the drunkard's pleasure in drink or in the saints' meditation that sweetness only, then you have got the truth, and then alone you will know what happiness means, what peace means, what love means. But as long as you keep these vain distinctions, silly, childish, foolish superstitions, all sorts of misery will come. That immortal One, the effulgent One, He is the background of the whole universe, it is all His sweetness. This body is a miniature universe, as it were; and through all the powers of the body, all the enjoyments of the mind, shines that effulgent One. That self-effulgent One who is in the body, He is the *Âtman.* "This world is so sweet to all beings, and every being is so sweet to it !"—for the self-effulgent Immortal One, is the bliss in this world. In us also, He is that bliss. He is the *Brahman.* "This air is so sweet to all beings, and all beings are so sweet to this air"—for He who is that self-effulgent immortal Being is the air ; He is also in this body. He is expressing Himself as the life of all beings. "This sun is so sweet to all beings, and all beings are so sweet to this sun," for He who is the self-effulgent Being is the sun, and Him we reflect as smaller lights. What can there be but His reflection ? He is in the body, and it is His reflection which makes us see the light. "This moon is so sweet to all beings, and all beings are so sweet to this moon," for that self-effulgent and immortal One who is the soul of that moon, He is in us expressing himself as mind. "This lightning is so sweet to all beings and all beings are sweet to this lightning," for the self-effulgent and immortal One is the soul of this lightning, and is also in us, because all is that *Brahman*. This *Brahman*, this *Âtman*, this Self, is the King of all beings. These ideas are very helpful to men ; they are for meditation. For instance, meditate on the earth, think of the earth, at the same time knowing that we have in us that which is in the earth, that both are the same. Identify the body with the earth, and identify the soul with the Soul behind. Identify the air with the soul that is in the air and that is in you and so on. All these are one, manifested in different forms. To realize this unity is the end and aim of all meditation, and this is what *Yajnavalkya* was trying to explain to *Maitreyi*.

VII

THE HIGHEST IDEAL OF JNÂNA YOGA

As this is the last of these classes it is better that I give a brief *resumé* of all that I have been trying to tell you. In the Vedas and Upanishads we find records of some of the very earliest religious ideas of the Hindus, ideas that long antedated the time of Kapila, ancient as this great sage is. He did not propound the *Sânkhya* philosophy as a new theory of his own. His task was to throw the light of his genius on the vast mass of religious theories that were existing in his time and bring out a rational and coherent system. He succeeded in giving India a psychology that is accepted to the present day by all the diverse and seemingly opposing philosophical systems to be found among the Hindus. His masterly analysis and his comprehensive statement of the processes of the human mind have not yet been surpassed by any later philosopher and he undoubtedly laid the foundation for the Advaita philosophy, which accepted his conclusions as far as they went and then pushed them a step farther, thus reaching a final unity beyond the duality that was the last word of the *Sânkhyas.*

Among all the religious ideas that preceded the time of Kapila,—I mean among recognized religious ideas, and not the very low ones, which do not deserve the name of religion,—we find, even the very first groups include the idea of inspiraton, and a revealed book and so forth. In the earliest stage, the idea of creation is very peculiar ; it is that the whole universe was created out of zero, by the will of God, that in the beginning this universe did not exist, and out of nothingness all this has come. In the next stage we find this conclusion questioned. The first step in Vedânta asks this question : How can existence be produced out of non-existence ? If this universe is existent it must have come out of something, because it was easy for them of old to see that there is nothing anywhere coming out of nothing, that all work that is being done by human hands requires materials. Naturally, therefore, the ancient Hindus rejected the first idea that this world was created out of nothing, and sought some material out of which this world was created. The whole history of religion, in fact, is the search for this material in our attempts to answer the question : Out of what has all this been produced ? Apart from the question of the efficient cause or God, apart from the question whether God created the universe, the great question of all questions has been, out of what did God create it ? All the philosophies are turning, as it were, on this question.

One solution is that this material and God and soul are eternal existences, like three parallel lines running eternally side by side, of which nature and soul comprise what they call the dependent, and God the independent Being. Every soul, like every particle of matter, is perfectly dependent on the will of God. These and many other ideas we find already existing when the *Sânkhya* psychology was brought forward by Kapila. According to it, perception comes by the transmission of the suggestion,—which causes irritation of the physical doors of the organs viz. perception first to the eyes etc.,—from the eyes etc. to the organs, from the organs to the mind, from the mind to the *buddhi* and from the *buddhi* to something which is a unit, which they call the *Âtman*. Coming to modern physiology we know that they have found centres for all the different sensations. First are found the lower centres, then a higher grade of centres, and these two will exactly correspond with the actions of the *buddhi* and the *manas* (mind), but not one centre has been found which controls all the other centres, so philosophy cannot answer what unifies all these centres. Where and how do the centres get unified ? The centres in the brain are all different, and there is not one centre which controls all the others ; therefore, so far as it goes, the *Sânkhya* psychology stands unchallenged upon this point. We must have this unification, something upon which the sensations will be reflected, to form a complete whole. Until there is that something, I cannot have any idea of you, or the picture, or anything else. If we had not that unifying something we would only see, then after a while hear, and then feel, and while we heard a man talking, we should not see him at all, because all the centres are different.

This body is made of particles which we call matter, and it is dull and insentient. So is what is called the fine body. The fine body, according to the *Sânkhyas* is a little body, made of very fine particles, so fine that no microscope can see them. What is the use of it? It is the receptacle of what we call mind. Just as this gross body is the receptacle of the grosser forces, so the fine body is the receptacle of of the finer forces, that which we call thought with its various modifications. First is the body, which is gross matter, with gross force. Force cannot exist without matter for it can manifest itself only through matter ; so the grosser forces work through the body and finally become finer. The very force which is working in a gross form works in a fine form and becomes thought.

There is no real difference between them, simply one is the gross and the other the fine manifestation of the same thing. Neither is there any difference is substance between the fine body and the gross body. The fine body is also material, only very fine material.

Whence do all these forces come? According to the Vedânta philosophy there are two things which form nature, one of which they call *Âkâsa*, which is substance, or matter, infinitely fine, and the other they call *Prâna*. Whatever you see, or feel, or hear, as air or earth, or anything, is material. And everything is a form of this *âkâsa*. It becomes finer and finer, or grosser and grosser, and it changes under the action of *Prâna* (universal Energy). Like *âkâsa prâna* is omnipresent, interpenetrating everything. *Akâsa* is like the water, and everything else in the universe like blocks of ice, made out of that water and floating in it, and *prâna* is the power that changes the *âkâsa* into all these various forms. This body is the instrument made out of *âkâsa* for the manifestation of *prâna* in gross forms, as muscular motion, or walking, sitting, talking and so on. The fine body also is made of *âkâsa*, a much finer form of *âkâsa*, for the manifestation of the same *prâna* in the finer form of thought. So, first there is this gross body, beyond that is the fine body, and beyond that is the *jiva* (soul), the real man. Just as these finger nails can be pared off a hundred times a year, and yet are still a part of our bodies, not different, so we have not two bodies. It is not that man has a fine and also a gross body ; it is the one body, only it remains longer when it is a fine body, and the grosser it is the sooner it dissolves. Just as I can cut this nail a hundred times a year, so millions of times I can shed this body is one æon, but the fine body will remain. According to the dualists this *jiva*, or the real man, is very fine, minute.

So far we have seen that man is a being who has first a gross body which dissolves very quickly, then a fine body which remains through æons, and lastly a *jiva*. This *jiva*, according to the Vedânta philosophy, is eternal, just as God is eternal, and *Prakriti* is also eternal, but changefully eternal. The materials of *Prakriti*, the *prâna* and the *âkâsa*, are eternal, but are changing into different forms eternally. Matter and force are eternal, but their combinations vary continually. The *jiva* is not manufactured, either of *âkâsa*, or of *prâna*; it is immaterial, and therefore will remain for ever. It is not the result of any combination of *prâna* and *âkâsa*, and whatever is not the result of combination will never be destroyed, because destruction is decomposion. That which is not a compound cannot be destroyed. The gross body is a compound of *âkâsa* ând *prâna* in various forms and will be decomposed. The fine body will also be decomposed after a long time, but the *jiva* is a simple, and will never be destroyed. For the same reason, we cannot say it ever was born. Nothing simple can be born; only that which is a compound can be born. The whole of this nature combined in these millions of forms is under the will of God. God is all pervading, omnicient, formless, everywhere, and He is directing this nature day and night. The whole of it is under His control. There is no independence of any being. It cannot be. He is the Ruler. This is the teaching of dualistic Vedânta.

Then the question comes, if God be the Ruler of this universe, why did He create such a wicked universe, why must we suffer so much? The answer is made that it is not God's fault. It is our own fault that we suffer. Whatever we sow that we reap. God does not do anything to punish us. If a man is born poor, or blind, or lame, he did something before he was born in that way, something that produced these results. The *jiva* has been existing for all time, was never created. It has been doing all sorts of things all the time. Whatever we do we suffer for. If we do good we shall have happiness, and if bad, unhappiness. This *jiva* is by its own nature pure, but ignorance covers its nature, says the dualist. As by evil deeds it has covered itself with ignorance, so by good deeds it can become conscious of its own nature again. Just as it is eternal, so its nature is pure. The nature of every being is pure. When through good deeds all its sins and misdeeds have been washed away, then the *jiva* becomes pure again, and when he becomes pure he goes after death by what is called *Devayana* (the path of the gods), to heaven, or the abode of the gods. If he has been only an oridinarily good man he goes to what is called the "Abode of the Fathers."

When the gross body falls, the organs of speech enter the mind. You cannot think without words; wherever there are words there must be thought. The mind is resolved into the *prâna*, and the *prâna* resolves into the *jiva*. Then the *jiva* leaves the body and goes to that condition of reward or punishment which he has earned by his past life. *Devaloka* is the "place (or abode) of the gods." The word *deva* (god) means bright or shining one, and corresponds to what the Christians and Mohammedans call "angels." According to this teaching there are various heavenly spheres somewhat analogous to the various heavens described by Dante in the *Divine Comedy*. There are the heaven of the fathers (or *pitris*), *devaloka*, the lunar sphere, the electric sphere and highest of all the *Brahmaloka*, the heaven of *Brahma*. From all the lower heavens the *jiva* returns again to human birth, but he who attains to *Brahmaloka* lives there through all eternity. These are the highest men who have become perfectly unselfish, perfectly purified, who have given up all desires, do not want to do anything except to worship and love God. There is a second class, who do good works, but want some reward, want to go to heaven in return. When they die, their *jiva* goes to the lunar sphere, where it enjoys and becomes a *deva* (god or angel). The gods, the *devas*, are not eternal, they have to die. In heaven they will all die. The only deathless place is *Brahmaloka*, where alone there is no birth and no death. In our mythology it is said there are also the demons, who sometimes give the gods chase. In all mythologies you read of these fights between the demons, or wicked angels, and the gods and sometimes the demons conquer the gods. In all mythologies also, you find that the *devas* were fond of the beautiful daughters of men. As a *deva*, the *jiva* only reaps results of past actions, but makes no new Karma. Karma means actions that will produce effects, also those effects, or results of action. When a man dies and becomes a *deva* he has a period of pleasure, and during that time makes no fresh Karma; he simply enjoys the reward of his past good works. But when the good Karma is worked out then the other Karma begins to take effect.

In the Vedas there is no mention of hell. But afterwards the *purânas*, the later books in our Scriptures, thought that no religion could become complete without a proper attachment of hells, and so they invented all sorts of hells, with as many, if not more, varieties of punishment than Dante saw in his *Inferno*, but our books are merciful enough to say that it is only for a period. Bad Karma is worked out in that state and then the souls come back to earth and get another chance. This human form is the great chance. It is called the *karmic* body, in which we decide our fate. We are running in a huge circle, and this is the point in the circle which determines the future. So a human body is considered the greatest body there is; man is greater than the gods. Even they return to human birth. So far with dualistic Vedânta.

Next comes a higher conception of Vedânta philosophy, which says that these ideas are crude. If you say there is a God who is an infinite Being, and a soul which is also infinite, and *Prakriti* which is also infinite, you can go on multiplying infinites indefinitely, but that is illogical, because each would limit the other and there would be no real infinite. God is both the material and the efficient cause of the universe; He projects this universe out of Himself. Does that mean that God has become these walls, and this table, that God has become the animal, the murderer, and all the evils in the world? God is pure, how can He become all these degenerate things? He has not. God is unchangeable, and all these changes are in *Prakriti*,—just as I am a soul and have a body; this body is not different from me in a sense, yet I, the real "I," in fact am not this body. For instance, I am a child, I become a young man, an old man, but my soul has not changed. It remains the same soul. Similarly the whole universe, comprised of *Prakriti*, and and infinite number of souls, is, as it were, the infinite body of God. He is interpenetrating the whole of it. He alone is unchangeable, but *Prakriti* changes and the souls too change. In what way does *Prakriti* change? In its forms; it takes fresh forms. But the souls cannot change that way. They contract and expand in knowledge. Every soul contracts by evil deeds. Those deeds which contract the natural knowledge and purity of the soul are called evil deeds. Those deeds, again, which bring out the natural glory of the soul, are called good deeds. All these souls were pure, but they have become contracted by their own acts. Still, through the mercy of God, and by doing good deeds, they will expand and become pure again. Every soul has the same chance, and, in the long run, must become pure and free itself from *Prakriti*. But this universe will not cease, because it is infinite. This is the second theory. The first is called dualistic Vedânta ; while the second which teaches that there is God, soul, and *Prakriti*, that soul and *Prakriti* form the body of God, and that these three form the unit—is called qualified monistic Vedânta. Believers in this second theory are called qualified non-dualists (*Visishtadvaitins*).

The last and highest theory is pure monism, or as it is known in India, *Advaita*. It also teaches that God must be both the material and the efficient cause of this universe. As such, God has become the whole of this universe. This theory denies that God is the soul, and the universe is the body, and the body is changing. In that case what is the use of calling God the material cause of this universe ? The material cause is the cause become effect ; the effect is nothing but the cause in another form. Wherever you see effect, it is the cause reproduced. If the universe is the effect, and God the cause, this must be the reproduction of God. If it be claimed that the universe is the body of God and that that body becomes contracted and fine and becomes the cause, and out of that the universe is evolved, then the *advaitist* says it is God Himself who has become this universe. Now comes a very fine question. If God has become this universe, then everything is God. Certainly; everything is God. My body is God, and my mind is God, and my soul is God. Then why are there so many *jivas*? Has God become divided into millions and millions of *jivas*? How can that infinite power and substance, the one Being of the universe become divided? It is impossible to divide infinity. How can the pure Being become this universe? If He has become the universe, He is changeful, and if He is changeful, He is in *Prakriti*, and whatever is in *Prakriti* is born and dies. If

God is changeful, He must die some day. Remember that. Again, how much of God has become this universe ? If you say "X," the algebraical unknown quantity, then God is God minus "X" now, and therefore not the same God as before this creation, because so much of Him has become this universe. The answer of the monist is that this universe has no real existence, it exists in appearance only. These *devas* and gods and angels and being born and dying, and all these infinite number of souls coming up and going down, all these things are mere dreams. All is the one Infinite. The one sun reflected on various drops of water appears to be many. Millions of globules of water reflect so many millions of suns and in each globule there is a perfect image of the sun, yet there is only sun, one—so it is with all these *jivas,* they are but reflections of the one infinite Being. A dream cannot be without a reality, and that reality is the one infinite Existence. You, as body, mind, or soul, are a dream, but what you really are is Existence-Knowledge-Bliss Absolute. Thus says the *Advaitist*. All these births and rebirths, this coming and going are but parts of the dream. You are infinite. Where can you go? The sun, moon, and the whole universe are but a drop in your nature. How can you be born or die? The Self was never born, never will be born, never had father or mother, friends or foes, for it is Existence-Knowledge-Bliss Absolute.

What is the goal, according to this philosophy? To receive this knowledge and become one with the universe. For them who attain to this, all heavens, even *Brahmaloka*, are destroyed, the whole dream vanishes, and they find themselves the eternal God of the universe. They attain their real individuality, infinitely beyond these little selves which we now think of so much importance. No individuality will be lost; an infinite and eternal Individuality will be realized. Pleasure in little things will cease. We are finding pleasure in this little body, in this little individuality but how much greater the pleasure will be when this whole universe appears as our own body? If there be pleasure in these separate bodies, how much more when all bodies are one? The man who has realized this has attained to freedom, has gone beyond the dream and known himself in his real nature. This is the teaching of Advaita, the non-dualistic Vedânta.

These are the three steps which Vedânta philosophy has taken, and we cannot go beyond, because we cannot go beyond unity. When any science reaches a unity it cannot possibly go any farther. You cannot go beyond the idea of the

Absolute, the idea of the One, out of which everything in the universe, has evolved. All people cannot take up this *Advaita* philosophy ; it is too hard. First of all, it is very difficult to understand it intellectually. It requires the sharpest of intellects, a bold understanding. Secondly, it does not suit the vast majority of people.

It is better to begin with the first of these three steps. Then by thinking of that and understanding it, the second one will open of itself. Just as a race travels, so individuals have to travel. The steps which the human race has taken to come to the highest pinnacle of religious thought, every individual will have to take. Only, while the human race took millions of years to reach from one step to another, individuals may live the whole life of the human race in a few years, or they may be able to do it more quickly, perhaps in six months. But each one of us will have to go through these steps. Those of you who are non-dualists can, no doubt, look back to the period of your lives when you were strong dualists. As soon as you think you are a body and a mind, you will have to accept the whole of this dream. If you have one piece you must take the whole. The man who says, here is this world but there is no God, is a fool, because if there be a world there will have to be a cause of the world, and that is what is called God. You cannot have an effect without knowing that there is a cause. God will only vanish when this world vanishes. When you have realized your one-ness with God, this world will no longer be for you. As long as this dream exists, however, we are bound to look upon ourselves as being born and dying, but as soon as the dream that we are bodies vanishes, so will vanish this dream that we are being born and dying, and so will vanish the other dream that there is a universe. That very thing which we now see as this universe will appear to us as God, and that very God who was so long external, will appear as the very Self of our own selves. The last word of *Advaita* is, *Tat tvam asi*,—"That thou art."

Published by

Facsimile Publisher
Ashok Vihar, Delhi-110052 (India)
Website: www.facsimilepublisher.com

Distributed by

Gyan Books Pvt. Ltd.
5, Ansari Road, Daryaganj, New Delhi-110002 (India)
E-mail: books@gyanbooks.com, Website: www.gyanbooks.com

8 888000 519881